The Frugal Fly Fisherman

Bending the Rod without Breaking the Bank

PATRICK STRAUB

D1569337

LYONS PRESS

Guilford, Connecticut

An imprint of Globe Pequot Press

To any angler who has the patience to teach someone.
The future of our sport is in your hands.

Lyons Press is an imprint of Globe Pequot Press.

Project editor: David Legere
Text design: Sheryl Pirolo Kober
Layout artist: Melissa Evarts

Photos by Patrick Straub unless otherwise noted.

Library of Congress Cataloging-in-Publication data is available on file.

ISBN 978-1-59921-999-8

Printed in the United States of America

10 9 8 7 6 5 4 3 2 1

Contents

Acknowledgments

Countless thanks go out to my editor, Allen Morris Jones, David Legere, and to all the great folks at Globe Pequot Press.

Huge thanks to Garrett Munson, Moe Witschard, Montana Troutfitters, Stephen Weisberg, Matson Rogers, Lee Kinsey, Chris Strainer, Mike Hoiness, Art Meripol, Paul Meripol, Mike Guerin, Matt McMeans, Judson Conway, Peter Crumbaker, John and Rebecca Shirley, Kris Kumlien, Peter McDonald, Michael Gracie, Alex Sansosti, Andy Sabota, Marshall Cutchin, Jeff Shrader, and the hundreds of fishing clients who drew the short straw and still chose to be in my boat.

A huge thanks to my parents, Del and Carolyn, for their love and support.

And the best for last: Thanks to my amazing wife, Brandy Moses; she is the greatest.

Chapter 1

What the Fly Fishing Establishment Doesn't Want You to Know

Sparkling rivers. Snowcapped peaks. Far-off saltwater flats. To mention fly fishing is to conjure up images of pristine waters and wild shores. But along with these picturesque landscapes are also less attractive snapshots of affluence and pretension, of sportsmen who take themselves perhaps too seriously. Most of us simply want to be in a place where water, fish, and fly can all come together, where we can forget the daily grind for a few moments. The best things in life truly are free. Or at least cheap.

So why does fly fishing often look so expensive?

For many, fly fishing is a romantic notion. Names like Alaska, the Bahamas, and Patagonia are used to sell rods, trips, guides, and gear, even though most fly anglers may never venture to any of these destinations. Think of it like the shiniest new car in the showroom. Of course we would all love that car, and most of us can even come up with several rationalizations why we might need it. Some of us could probably afford it, but do we really need it to get to work or to feel safe or to enjoy a drive?

Leaky waders? If you don't need them for a while, fill them with water to find the leaks. Then use your factory wader-repair kit.

Fly fishing is similar—there are rods made with technology rooted in space shuttles, but are they 100 percent necessary? Absolutely not. Are they fun to fish and use? Of course. Would we all love to have them? Probably. Have people been fly fishing for years without them? Yes.

Before the fly-fishing industry exploded in the mid-1990s, anglers fished all over the world with gear that we would now consider subpar. The rods and reels that were used to land the first hundred-pound tarpon on a fly or to entice the first finicky spring creek trout could not even be found today. Rods were made from any wood available, constantly breaking and difficult to cast. Flies were similar today, but tied on hooks that would rust after a few uses. And technical clothing like Gore-Tex and felt soles had not been invented.

Stick to It: Take some hot glue, a pair of old tennis shoes, and some replacement felt and create your own wading boots. This won't last forever, but will work for a while.

But having access to more sophisticated gear comes at a cost. Whether you are fishing with high-modulus graphite or Gore-Tex rain jackets and breathable waders, fly fishing's technological advances have spiked the *potential* price tag substantially. If you are fishing on a budget, the trick is knowing how and where to most efficiently place your hard-earned dollars.

These same advances that have made the sport more expensive have also made it more accessible, which has increased the demand for a wider array of products. Counterintuitively, then, most gear manufacturers and shops can now produce and sell gear across all price levels, catering not only to the high-dollar shoppers but to the frugal fly fishermen as well. If there ever were a time in the history of fly fishing to be frugal, it's now. The plethora of manufacturers and the number of local fly-fishing retailers serve up numerous options for penny pinchers to enjoy the sport.

But how do you wade through all the glossy advertisements and fishing shows, the latest technological advances, to find the necessary gear, that perfect balance of affordability and utility? And what is the necessary gear?

This book will show obvious bias for supporting your local fly-fishing specialty shop. These businesses are dedicated to your satisfaction and your growth as an angler, and they create customer loyalty by offering advice and gear for all levels and budgets. Most owners of fly-fishing stores feel a personal connection to their customers. Whether that connection comes in hiring their services for instruction or guided fishing or providing personal advice on choosing the right gear, it is a frugal decision to take advantage of the free advice from your local store.

A fly rod is your most important angling tool. Choose wisely.

If you are making your first visit to a local shop, prepare to be surprised. You are no doubt going to be staring at enough rods, reels, fly lines, gadgets, do-hickeys, and thing-ma-jobs to make you rethink your retirement strategy. But if you know how to ask the right questions, if you're humble and are forthcoming about your level of expertise and your budget, the educated staff of your local store will prove invaluable. In return, the staff will most certainly ask you some questions as well. "How much fishing do you think you will do?" Or, "What is your budget?" Or maybe, "Do you know where you will do most of your fishing?" Answer honestly. If you don't, then the expertise of the shop staff will be wasted.

But before you can begin to shop for gear, you need a thorough understanding of exactly what type of gear you will need and just how much to spend. So let's break it down.

First, you will need a fly-fishing rod. Whether you are fishing for trout or tarpon, for between $100 and $300 you can purchase a good quality rod that will cast well, look and feel nice, and most likely come with a guarantee. That may seem like a lot at first, but keep in mind you are going to purchase a rod that will last you several years, perhaps even a lifetime. Do a little math and that $300 rod, amortized over the course of a few hundred days on the water, just cost you a lot less.

Second, you will need a fly-fishing reel. For between $50 and $200 you can get a reel that will do everything you need it to do. But whether you spend $50 or $200 depends on where you will be doing most of your fishing. If you plan to fish saltwater, you are going to spend more. Most saltwater reels are larger and have a more durable drag system. These reels last longer in the harsh saltwater environment, but are more costly.

Third, you will need a fly line. For *most* fly-fishing situations, the rod is the most important element of your gear. But in *all* fly-fishing situations your fly line is *always* the second most important element. A fly line that slides through the guides well makes casting more efficient.

Lastly, you will need terminal tackle—leaders, flies, fly floatant, forceps, and a few other tools. Additional items like technical clothing, sunglasses, gear bags, and everything else under the sun are considerations as well.

A rod, reel, and line package that will fish well and hold up for several years shouldn't set you back more than $400, tops. You can always spend less, of course, but you will certainly get less.

Let's do a little comparison, and start by breaking down a typical day of fishing on a stretch of water within a 60-mile round-trip of your home. For these comparisons let's assume you already own a rod, reel, and fly line.

Gadgets are easy to find, but flies are the most crucial element in your terminal tackle.

Don't spend a lot of money on the camera you'll take with you fishing—water and electronics don't mix. With technology today most cell phones will take great pictures. The camera on the right cost $50 and takes great shots.

Mileage and gas: $20

Flies used while fishing: $10

Leaders and floatant: $5

Sandwich you made at home the night before: $5

Total: $40 for a day of fly fishing

Second, let's compare your $40 to some other popular activities such as golf, skiing, hiking, and four-wheeling. Lastly, we'll compare the approximate overhead of each activity:

Golf

Mileage and gas to course: $5

Green fees for 18 holes: $35

Golf balls: $10

Sandwich you made at home the night before: $5

Beers or cocktails from the club cart: $5 (Be realistic here. When that club cart comes rolling around you won't be able to resist.)

Total: $60

Skiing

Mileage and gas to ski hill: $20

Lift ticket: $50

Sandwich you made the night before: $5

Latte or cocktail pre- or post-skiing: $5

Total: $80

Hiking

Mileage and gas to trailhead: $20

Sandwich you made the night before: $5

Total: $25

All-Terrain Vehicle (ATV) Riding

Mileage and gas to trailheads: $20

Gas while riding: $10

Sandwich you made the night before: $5

Total: $35

Now the overhead comparisons:

Golf: A set of golf clubs runs upward from $150.

Skiing: A pair of skis runs upward from $300.

Hiking: A good pair of boots runs upward from $50.

Four-wheeling: An ATV starts at $3,000.

Once you take into account overhead, fly fishing looks a little less spendy.

But it's one thing to know intellectually that fly fishing is inexpensive; it's another thing entirely to know it in your gut, especially when you are in the fly shop staring at dozens of rods, deciding which one to purchase. But the process of starting out *and* being frugal shouldn't be intimidating or overwhelming. It could be if you try to go it alone, but this is where it saves to shop at your local fly shop.

Local fly shops and local fly fishing clubs are a great resource for free classes or instruction. Here students are learning to tie a popular local pattern.

www.MontanaTroutfitters.com

Across the country there are big-box sporting goods chain stores near the newest strip malls. Granted, they may have a large selection of equipment across all price ranges, but by choosing to purchase your gear at a big-box store rather than a local store, you lose the potential for long-term benefit from both you and the store.

A small retail store has a vested interest in your growth and loyalty to the sport. They rely on you as a customer. Of course they need sales volume and would love to sell a big-ticket item, as any smart business owner would. But whether you are looking for a $200 starter outfit or a $900 bar-stock limited edition reel made from parts of Sputnik, your local shop, day in and day out, is still going to be the best resource for your frugality.

If you are a dedicated customer to them, they are going to be dedicated to you. Most local shops offer free or highly reduced prices on classes. They also offer customer loyalty programs and weekly newsletters or sales updates. These will save you money. Most of all, they offer information: tips about local fishing spots, which fly patterns to use, perhaps even a little in-shop instruction. Most local shops pride themselves in offering the best information around and freely giving that information to anyone who wants it. Most shop owners don't expect anything in return for giving out such information, but as a frugal angler, don't allow your stinginess to keep you from politely reciprocating. It is always a good idea to give a little kickback—even if that means spending $5 on a few flies. In most instances it is the gesture more than the amount you lay on the counter that ensures the shop staff will be happy to see you the next time you are in.

Fishing is not meant to be complicated. Less is often more. Beyond the essential elements of a rod, reel, fly line, flies, and a small assortment of terminal tackle and peripherals, everything else is a luxury. And indeed, quite often, within the self-limitations of a budget lie any number of opportunities that might not otherwise have been explored.

No matter where you live, for instance, there are almost always fishing opportunities within a day's commute. Many species of fish are closer to home than might be expected. From bluegills to crappies to bass to carp, not all fly fishing has to be with trout or tarpon in mind.

A frugal fly fisherman doesn't covet information but does seek it out. Fly fishing is a pastime meant to be shared. Fly shops, angling clubs, Internet forums, and other social avenues are available for information, gear, and camaraderie. To be truly frugal, you must invest time in building social connections and developing lasting relationships with angling companions. The knowledge gained can be passed down through the generations, and the bonds created are timeless.

In the camaraderie of fly fishermen, you'll also find reasons to embrace conservation and work toward restoration of fishing opportunities. There

Thumbs up! These anglers shopped local, learned local, and voilà!

is no possibility of sharing a beloved pursuit if the venue is degraded. The desire to leave a place better than previously found is essential. Ensure the enjoyment of current fishing opportunities is available for future generations. There are many ways you can help: pick litter you see streamside, donate a day of your time for a stream clean-up, or join your local Trout Unlimited chapter—and the list goes on.

Commit to a big spend every so often. What is a great meal without dessert? Being consistently frugal has its long-term advantages, and among these is the ability to splurge on occasion. Hire a guide, take notes, and learn a year's worth of knowledge in one day. Purchase a nice rain jacket that will last a lifetime. Invest in some quality breathable waders.

Lastly, don't take your fishing too seriously. Life is full of stresses and responsibilities. Fishing shouldn't be one of them.

Chapter 2

Gear You Want to Have and Gear You *Must* Have

Fly-fishing gear is a curse. Too much gear and you spend more time futzing with gadgets and do-hickies than you do fishing. Not enough gear and you grow frustrated because you're in a situation without something you need. Being a frugal fly fisher helps the gear dilemma because it forces you to choose between luxury and necessity.

A seasoned angler can prioritize gear into one small pack.

Matt McMeans; www.bighornkingfisher.com

How do you choose what gear to have and not to have? Paring down your gear arsenal takes years and years to master.

But sticking to a budget doesn't make choosing what to have and what to sacrifice any easier or any less intimidating. How do you know if you need the five-in-one knot-tying tool or the digital stream thermometer? Or, perhaps a $10 fanny pack or a $100 vest? Prioritize, and the gear debate takes care of itself.

Fly fishing requires a rod, reel, fly line, leader and tippet, and a fly. These are the bare bones. If you have the money, you can also buy waders and wading boots, a vest or wading pack, sunglasses, headwear, gear bags, a net, a thermometer, lanyard . . . and the list goes on.

Let's start with flies. Fish cannot tell what brand of fly rod you use or how expensive your waders cost, but they *can* see your fly. Flies have a direct connection to the fish. Because of this, it is necessary to understand the importance of using or tying quality flies. With frugality in mind, using flies that will catch fish presents a challenge.

Before the fly-fishing retail market exploded, the way to get flies on the cheap was to tie them yourself. In the long run tying your own flies is the most frugal way to fly fish. Once you take into account the time it takes

Necessities	Price Range	Includes	Price
Flies	$.75 to $5.00	Two dozen flies	$35
Tippet material	$2.50 to $15.00 per spool	Three tippet spools	$15
Leaders	$1.50 to $3.00 per leader	Five leaders	$10
Fly line	$35 to $75	Fly line	$50
Rod	$100 to $300	Rod	$200
Reel	$35 to $120	Reel	$80
Approx costs for all	**$390**	**Total:**	**$390**
Should Haves		**Price Range**	
Breathable waders		$100 to $300	
Rain jacket		$100 to $300	
Sunglasses		$40 to $200	
Hat or cap		$5 to $30	
Vest and/or pack		$30 to $150	
Approx costs for all		**$460**	
Nonessential Terminal Tackle		**Price Range**	
Fly floatant		$2 to $5	
Forceps/release tool		$10 to $20	
Nippers		$2 to $30	
Weight (split shot or putty)		$2 to $10	
Strike indicators		$1 to $3	
Approx costs for all		**$30**	

to purchase the fly-tying equipment and then become proficient enough to tie flies that will fool fish, you may want to consider purchasing flies from a wholesale distributor or your local fly shop. There is a big downside to buying flies from a distributor rather than tying them yourself or buying them locally. Depending on where you live, if you buy locally or invest time in tying them yourself, you gain the ability to create custom patterns for specific waters. This can prove priceless if a certain bug is hatching or a certain baitfish is swimming. In most fishing situations the standard flies and sizes will work fine.

Because of the plethora of ways to obtain flies (Internet, local fly shop, or by tying them yourself) and the abundance of proven patterns, deciding where to buy and how much to spend on your fly selection is actually easier than choosing which rod or reel to purchase. Once you learn the fly patterns you will be using, it is a simple matter of learning to tie a few flies or shell out a few bucks to get what you need to catch some fish.

After flies, you need to decide on a tippet section and leader. In some instances the tippet and leader are one and the same. With the invention of knotless tapered leaders a few decades ago, anglers were able to fish a leader that already included a tippet section. Most anglers use a knotless tapered leader and then tie onto that a section of tippet material.

Why is this important to the frugal fly fisher? Because nothing is more frustrating than fooling a fish only to have it break off because of poor-quality tippet or leader material.

There are several good manufacturers out there, including Rio, Scientific Anglers, Dan Bailey's, Orvis, and Climax. But after deciding on a brand (every angler has a personal preference, which will only come to you

Leader options and tippets are plentiful. You will develop your favorite choices for materials and lengths.

with experience), you will need to make a decision with regard to fluorocarbon. Having been around since the mid-1990s, fluorocarbon has stood the test of time and is now widely available. Fluorocarbon will cost more, but you *might* find a little more success with it versus monofilament.

If you are doing a lot of subsurface fishing, use fluorocarbon instead of monofilament. Professional guides and anglers swear by fluorocarbon for underwater applications. You should, too.

Monofilament is the longtime standard in tippet and leader material. An abundance of manufacturers are making quality monofilament leaders, so the prices are substantially lower than fluorocarbon. Monofilament is also more appropriate in certain fly-fishing situations.

Because fluorocarbon is designed to sink, it's poor with flies that float, especially small flies. If the bulk of your fishing will be on the surface, then you can save a little bit of cash by buying monofilament instead of fluorocarbon.

Additionally, do not buy fluorocarbon leaders for most fishing situations; only buy fluorocarbon tippet material. Fluorocarbon leaders should be used when you want your leader to sink, and sink fast. But in a given day of fishing, you may want a slow sinking leader or a floating leader, so keep it simple and use monofilament leaders. When you want your leader to sink, add fluorocarbon tippet material to the end of your monofilament leader. There is a myth floating around out there that you cannot tie fluorocarbon to monofilament. As long as your knots are tied well, you have nothing to worry about joining fluorocarbon to monofilament.

Soap and Water: A little rinse after each day of fishing, whether fresh or salt, with mild soap and water dramatically increases the life of your gear.

As for leaders, over the long term, say a season or two, you are money ahead if you buy multipacks of leaders in a few lengths and sizes and then have a selection of tippet spools in various sizes. For example, buy several packs of 9-foot 5X leaders and be sure to have spools of tippet in sizes 3X, 4X, 5X, and 6X. This allows you to add, or cut, your 9-foot 5X leader to match the fishing situation. By having a selection of tippet, you can add

Fly-fishing gadgets can quickly take over your gear arsenal. Here are the essential accessories for most fishing situations. Clockwise: dry fly powder (to dry saturated flies); moldable weight; fly floatants (gel and liquid); strike indicators (pinch-ons and floating bubbles); and split shot for weight.

to the end of your leader to maintain its length without having to use a whole new leader.

Next to a good pair of polarized sunglasses, your fly line may be the most overlooked piece of reasonably priced equipment. Similar to your flies, a good fly line will increase your fishing success. You wouldn't buy a Ferrari and put Walmart tires on it. So why spend your hard-earned dollars on a nice fly rod and use a cheap fly line? A high-quality fly line will upgrade any rod.

For around $50 all fly line manufacturers have quality lines that are durable and cast well. But don't stop caring about your fly line the moment you cease fishing. Be sure to clean it after each use and also apply line dressing more often than not—about once every five to six days of fishing is a good idea. These simple steps will ensure your line will last several years. A quality, clean fly line can add a lot to an expensive fly rod—even an $800 fly rod can't cast well with a dirty, poor-quality fly line.

From fly to tippet to leader to fly line, the gear that is truly "on the water" is continually replaced. Hopefully it's being replaced because you are catching fish and not trees or your angling companion. These items are often called "terminal tackle" because their use in fishing results in their replacement. But because they "make the connection" between you and the fish, they are not to be overlooked.

When taking a closer look at costs, flies range from $0.75 to $5.00 apiece. Tippet material costs anywhere from $2.50 to $15.00 for a spool, depending on type (fluorocarbon or mono) and quantity of tippet in the spool. Leaders cost around $3.00 a piece, sometimes less, sometimes more. But a three-pack of 9-foot leaders should cost around $12.00. A quality fly line shouldn't cost more than $70.00, but for around $50.00 you can get one that will do the job well and last a few seasons. Any fly line less than $30.00 will probably make you wish you had splurged a little.

Firm Footing: Take your felt or non-slip wading boots and carefully drill small holes *only* into the felt and base of the boot. Next, thread the holes with a threader. When you need cleats, use small screws. You now have two pairs of boots instead of one, saving you money.

For any frugal fly fisher, splurging is allowed—you have to treat yourself at some point. When creating a budget for your fly-fishing gear, consider spending a good chunk of your budget on your rod. Of all the necessities (rod, reel, line, flies, leaders, and tippet), the rod will be your most expensive purchase. But it is also the piece of equipment most likely to stay with you over the long haul.

Purchasing a rod used to be a simple process. There were only a few manufacturers and even fewer places to buy them. Today, buying a rod can be a cumbersome process—it is probably easier to just ask for a rod as a gift and let someone else do all the legwork!

A good way to get free advice on not only rod selection but also fishing information is to invest considerable time in shopping for a rod. Patience and knowledge during the rod-buying process will pay huge dividends when you hit the water.

An expensive reel is essential in very few fly-fishing situations. Even if you are chasing tarpon in the Florida Keys or fishing 7X tippet to 20-inch rising trout on a Montana spring creek, most fly-fishing situations call for a quality reel, but not necessarily the most expensive. Despite their necessity in fly fishing, the main purpose of a reel is storing excess fly line and to allow line to come off the reel when a fish is making a run away from you.

Quality in a reel first and foremost means that it has a decent drag system and parts that are protected from grit and grime. Ideally a disc drag system is preferred, but many big fish have been landed on reels with non-disc drag systems.

Durability is important, perhaps even more than drag mechanics. Often the durability of a reel can be felt by fondling the reel in the store—if it feels strong in your hand, then it most likely is.

Armed with a pocket full of flies, a well-tied leader, a lubricated fly line, your rod, and a reel, you are now ready to hit the water. Whether you are heading to a saltwater flat or beach or jetty, a stream or a larger river, or a lake or pond, you've got the tools to catch some fish. Could you have more tools? Obviously. Breathable waders, wading boots, sunglasses, a stripping basket, and other items could be added to your arsenal.

Instead of a vest, use a fishing shirt with large chest pockets. From fly boxes to snacks to sunscreen, a lot of things will fit in these pockets.

Andy Sabota; www.midwestflyworks.com

No matter how small or how big a water you plan to fish, a pair of breathable waders and quality wading boots will increase your fishing opportunities.

A pair of breathable waders is almost a must for any angler living north of Florida. Why aren't they a necessity, lumped in there with a rod, reel, and a fly line? Because most anglers do the bulk of their fishing during the warmer summer months when waders are not necessary. If you choose to invest in a pair, you will only increase the number of available fishing options.

From a frugal standpoint it makes sense to purchase waders—do the math: If you spend money on the necessities but only fish a few days out of the year, then you are not getting a true bang-for-your-buck. Plus some of the best fishing occurs in cooler weather or in cold-water environments.

Two types of waders are available—stockingfoot waders and bootfoot waders. Stockingfoot waders

> Don't buy a new pair of waders. Simply return them to the factory and they will repair or replace them, sometimes for free or for a nominal charge.

require you to also purchase wading boots. Bootfoot waders do not. Bootfoot waders have built-in wading boots attached to the foot of the wader. When evaluating the type of wader to purchase, think about where you will be doing most of your fishing.

If you fish shorelines or streams or swampy lakeshores, you will need a pair of sturdy wading boots to accompany your stockingfoot wad-

Tennis anyone? You can usually substitute an old pair of tennis shoes for wader boots. You're going to slip around on the rocks more, but slipperiness might be better than shelling out the $150 for a pair of dedicated wading boots.

ers. Oftentimes bootfoot waders do not have the stability of wading boots. Wading boots are designed for stability and traction. For wading rocky streams you need a pair of felt-soled wading shoes or, most recently, a pair

Art Meripol; www.artmeripol.com

Waders aren't always a necessity. Warmer weather allows for "wet-wading" or going without waders. If you only fish during the warmer months, you may not even need to purchase waders. But it does help to have a sturdy pair of wading boots.

Most waders today are very durable. Choose waders with reinforced legs, because you never know when you might need to bust through brush.

Breathable waders have made fly fishing much more enjoyable. They can be used in winter with lots of layers underneath but also work great in summer when all you need is one layer to keep you dry.

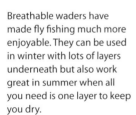

of non-slip rubber-soled wading shoes as a few states are in the process of outlawing felt. When the weather gets hot, you can shed the waders and wear your boots with shorts or pants and you still have the stability and traction of your boots.

One possible option for purchasing waders *and* wading boots together is a pair of bootfoot waders. For cold-weather fishing, bootfoots are the way to go because air is allowed to move around your foot and you don't have a wet boot around your stockingfoot waders.

You may be asking "What did people do before waders and wading shoes?" They wore thick wool pants or nylon or rubber waders and wore boots on the outside of those pants—roughing it by today's standards. Of course you can rough it, but ask yourself what is your priority—frugality or comfort and safety?

An often overlooked piece of equipment is a good pair of polarized sunglasses. They offer an aid to your fishing. By reducing glare they cut

High-quality sunglasses allow you to see more fish . . . and bring more fish to hand!

21

This angler has sun protection covered. Literally. Sungloves, a neck gaiter, and wide-brimmed hat; and even though you can't see it, you can be pretty sure he's well-lathered in sunscreen.

the reflection of the sun off the water, allowing you to see into the water—greatly increasing your ability to act as a predator to your targeted species. Polarized sunglasses also offer protection from errant fly casts—a surefire way to end a day's enjoyment is a fly in the eyeball. And they protect your eyes from harmful UV rays. Quality glasses can be had for a reasonable price. Your eyes are worth it.

Quality glasses typically have glass lenses or some other composite material that is scratch-proof or can be easily repaired if scratched. Look for lightweight frames with few moving parts. Try on a few pairs and choose the pair that fits you best.

Let's say you've now bought everything mentioned so far: flies, tippets, leaders, fly line, rod, reel, waders and wading boots, and sunglasses. What's next? If you own any shirts with big pockets and a baseball cap, you really are ready for just about anything. But you might also want a vest or pack to hold your gear. Over the past twenty years fishing vests and packs have been revolutionized. Much like how graphite and breathable waders have brought a whole new level of ease and enjoyment to rods and waders, synthetic fabrics are responsible for hundreds of vest or pack options.

The type of vest or pack you purchase should really be determined by the waters you plan to fish and personal preference. Time will tell what type of pack system you like clinging to your body. Chest packs are typically worn high while a "sling" system will drop to your side; other packs will rest at sternum level.

Fanny packs for fishing are being made with water bottle holders, multi-compartments, and more nooks and crannies and gear-holding do-hickies than you can shake a stick at. Be careful, though. These

This angler is armed for everything. By strapping on a backpack he can fish for the entire day.

extra-gadget holders may only do one thing well: snag your fly line. Still, a good fanny pack can be ideal for saltwater flats fishing or when wading within reasonable distance of a boat. Before the rush of synthetic materials slammed the fly-fishing market, a fanny pack was a cheap option. Now they can cost upwards of several hundred dollars.

Until the late 1990s "packs" didn't exist. Most fly fishers wore fishing vests. For many anglers vests are a solid option as they can hold a ton of gear. They may not be ideal for hot weather wading, because a vest is one more layer of clothing, but they are great for those anglers who want to keep nearly all of their gear in one place. Vests tend to be a little more expensive than chest or fanny packs.

If you plan to do a lot of hiking and fishing, look into a convertible backpack and chest or waist pack. Or go about it the old-school way—use a backpack and wear a fishing vest under your backpack. This is not a bad option because you can always drop the pack in the bushes, fish for a while, and then return to the pack as needed.

A quality rain jacket also works well to keep you warm in winter!

Depending on where and when you plan to fish, a rain jacket is a necessity. When considering a rain jacket, think long and hard about seasonality and pockets. If you plan to fish a lot in cool and wet weather, your rain jacket may also become part of your storage solution—a rain jacket with big front pockets is handy for fly boxes, tippet spools, and additional gear.

After every outing, no matter how deep you waded, hang your waders. Never stuff them in a bag and leave them for longer than a few hours. The humidity from the damp waders will cause mildew, which will cause seams to break down faster.

Gear, and its obtainment, can be both cumbersome and enjoyable. Most anglers progress through a cycle of wanting as much gear as possible before gradually confronting the dilemma of how to store it all. Manufacturers and sales reps love that process.

The frugal fly fisher educates herself about the types of gear available and evaluates the most important factors in the purchasing decision. If you only have $300 to spend, you need to be shrewd in the allocation of that money. It will vary from person to person.

Today's modern graphite rods can really be put to the test. This angler puts the "hurt-on" during a Missouri River rainbow's speedy run.

Chapter 3

Fly-Fishing Rod: A Paintbrush for Your Art or a Tool for Your Shed?

Norman Maclean writes in *A River Runs Through It*, "My father was very sure about certain matters pertaining to the universe. To him, all good things—trout as well as eternal salvation—come by grace and grace comes by art and art does not come easy."

In the days of Maclean's father, split cane and silk fly lines were the only tackle available. If art is meant to be difficult, then the art of fly fishing was perhaps easier to achieve with these less sophisticated tools. But in today's world of Gore-Tex, carbon-fibers, and high-modulus graphite, does any element of artistry remain to fly fishing? And if you are trying to be frugal, should you really care?

Whether fly fishing is viewed as an art or just a sport depends upon your perspective, but for the frugal fly fisher, there is certainly an art to getting the most for your dollar. Patience and education are paramount when buying gear, but practicality reigns when deciding how much to spend. You may wish to upgrade your existing fly rod, but is it practical if you don't plan on fishing any new locales? Perhaps you should consider selling your existing fly rod before buying an upgrade, particularly when it's off-season and you have time to shop around for the best bargain. "Test-driving" new rods is part of the fun of fly fishing. Ignore the latest "Five-Weight Shootout" and "Top Seven Dry Fly Rods"

Always, always, always put your rod back in your case when not in use. Not doing so is a recipe for a broken rod—and most manufacturers charge a replacement fee these days.

Few frugal anglers can afford bamboo rods, but for those who can, the rod's action is unique and enjoyable.

articles and just go cast a rod that looks like it might be a good fit with you and your personality.

Most rods available today are made of three possible materials: fiberglass, bamboo, or graphite. Each has its advantages, and each has its drawbacks.

Bamboo was the first mainstream (as mainstream as fly fishing could get) material used in fly fishing. Today a good bamboo rod is unaffordable. The only bamboo fly rods even considered by any frugal fly fisher would be those found in a pawn shop or a garage sale. And even if you were to get lucky and find such a rod, it most likely would be worth exactly what you paid for it. Gone are the days of pawn shops not knowing just how much rods are worth.

Post–World War II, glass rods came to the fly-fishing market. They were not around for long. By the time manufacturers began uncovering the unique qualities of fiberglass, in the 1970s, graphite exploded onto the scene. Lately, there has been a minor resurgence in fiberglass rods, the action of which is very distinct. Fiberglass rods offer a slow-action rod. When fighting a fish, the angler will feel the movement of a hooked fish well into the butt of the rod. Casting and fish-fighting just feel good on a fiberglass rod. For this reason fiberglass rods should tweak the attention of any frugal fly fisher. The downside is that very few fiberglass rod manufacturers are making frugal rods. If you are interested in dabbling with fiberglass, the Internet is a good place to start, but be prepared to do some soul-searching. The prices will test your frugal nature.

In the 1970s graphite allowed rod makers to build a rod that was lighter than fiberglass or bamboo. These rods caught on quickly with most anglers. Over the past thirty years, manufacturers have tapped into the wide array of graphite. The abundance and scope of material allow for a massive selection in price and style. In fact most manufacturers offer rods ranging from $150 to $1,500—the difference is typically in structure of the graphite.

If your rod did not come with a case, use PVC pipe to make your own. Pipe sections can be readily found at your local hardware store. Glue a cap on one end and a screw-on cap on the other end. Voila—rod case for under $25. Not incidentally, this type of homemade case also tends to be more secure. No one's going to break into a truck to steal a PVC pipe, but they might if they see a bright green Winston rod case.

Fiberglass rods are having a resurgence. Still priced too high for most frugal anglers, they are more novelty than practicality.

Andy Sabota; www.midwestflyworks.com

Graphite rods are reasonably priced, cast well, and come in hundreds of options and actions.

Sparing you the details of how graphite is created and rated, the lighter-weight, higher-modulus makeup graphite means a more expensive rod. But that doesn't mean that you cannot purchase a high-quality graphite rod for a good price. The various characteristics of the structure of graphite make it possible for manufacturers to offer rods that are enjoyable to fish for a fraction of what they cost ten, twenty, or even thirty years ago.

After considering material of the rod, the next factor in rod selection is line weight. If you are only going to purchase one rod (and most frugal fly fishers will only want to purchase one rod), line weight is crucial—you want a rod that you can use in most fishing situations.

Rods are made in various weights to coincide with their appropriate fly line. The weights start at 0 and go to 16. A 16-weight rod is the heaviest rod made today and is used in heavy-tackle, bluewater fishing situations. And until a few years back the lightest rod available was a 2-weight. Today, 0-weight rods are on the market, but fishing them is more of a gimmick than a necessity. There might be a time and a place for fishing a 0-weight rod, but frugal fly fishers are going to make do with less specialized equipment.

The rod in this illustration is only bending at the tip. Not great for feeling the movements of fish during the fight.

This angler's rod is bending in the middle. Better than the previous rod, but still not ideal for feeling all of the movements during a fight.

In this picture the rod is in full-flex mode. Heavy pressure can be put on a fish while the fish's movements are still. Rods that can bend this far down into their butt-section are ideal for fighting big fish.

Despite the abundance of available rod weights, most of the inexpensive rods are made in the 4-weight to 7-weight range. This is the range for most freshwater fly-fishing situations—whether you are pursuing trout, bass, panfish, steelhead, or carp, and whether you are fishing a high mountain stream, a farm pond, a large river, or a freshwater lake. To pinpoint the rod weight for your fishing, take the "What Rod Do I Really Need?" quiz at the end of this chapter.

Big Fish Require Big Bows: If you hook a big fish and it jumps out of the water, be sure to add some slack in the taut fly line with your rod. You do this by "bowing" or leaning forward with your arm extended like you were bending down to bow. If you don't, you just lost your fly . . . and the money you paid for it!

The next thing to consider is rod length. Rods run from 7 feet to 10 feet. Most rods that fall into the frugal category are 8.5 feet to 9 feet in length. The length of rod you choose is determined by where you expect to do most of your fishing. A general rule: If you plan to fish small creeks with thick brush cover, you want a shorter rod; if you plan to fish lakes, ponds, or larger rivers, opt for a longer rod, at least 8.5 feet.

Many anglers find they enjoy the fishing attributes of a longer rod over those of a shorter rod. Long rods often make mending and line-management easier, but sometimes feel a little clunkier while casting. If you enjoy casting a short rod, go with your gut. But honestly evaluate where you plan to do most of your fishing.

Rod length and weight are often related to the casting action of the rod. Action and taper are described as the "speed" of the rod. The casting action of a rod is also related to the "speed" of the rod during the casting stroke. Another way to view this is how the softness of the rod's tip relates to the cast. A faster rod is going to have a stiffer tip and a slower rod is going to have a softer tip. A stiffer tip will cast better in windy conditions, will cast heavier flies, and may handle fish a little better in the fight. Emphasis is on *may* because sometimes a stiffer tip can work against you.

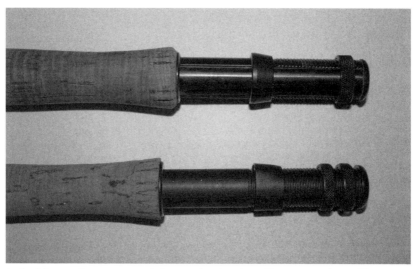

Both of these reel seats are on rods that cost less than $200. The top one is from a fifteen-year-old rod. Looks just as good as the brand-new one on the bottom.

A softer tip will allow for a more delicate presentation of your fly, will allow you to feel more of the rod's action when you cast, and provide more give while fighting a fish. Fortunately, nearly all manufacturers are now making rods with a tip action that falls somewhere in the middle between too soft and too stiff.

The last practical thing to consider is the quality of the hardware on the rod. The difference between rods that cost upward of $400 is often the quality of the guides and the rod handle. Once rods drop below a certain price (typically $200), the guides are often no longer anodized aluminum, the paint and finish aren't as durable or as attractive, and the reel seat usually lacks eye-catching wood grains. You will still get an anodized reel seat.

Mind Games: When fighting a fish, confuse them. Apply diagonal pressure with a good bend in the rod, and move them from side to side. The changing of directions keeps them guessing, which keeps them confused, thus making it easier to bring them to net quicker.

Nearly all rods sold today feature anodized reel seats. Here are two up-locking reel seats. The rod on the right also features a fighting butt—a must for most rods 8-weight and heavier.

Other characteristics that increase the cost of a rod? The style and color of the finish, wood used in the reel seat, and any engraving on the rod. Color and finish are not practical improvements and shouldn't be taken into account. The only time color should be considered is if a rod has an overly shiny finish. The shiny finish may reflect sunlight, which could possibly spook a fish.

Wood in a reel seat is pure luxury and doesn't add any practical value to the rod. While it is fun to look at the rod handle and see bird's eye maple or zebrawood or other grains, consider saving that money and using it for instruction or gas money for fishing.

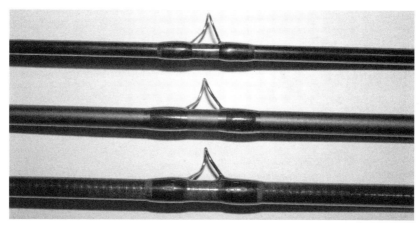

These three rods vary greatly in price. But can you tell which rod is the most expensive because of the snake guides? A pro might. If you can't, see below.

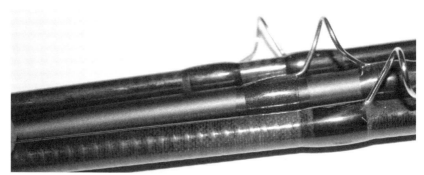

The top rod costs well over $700. The middle rod around $150. The bottom rod around $250. The difference? Very subtle—the top rod's guide is much thinner, making the rod lighter. The wrapping and finish are more durable as well. But will the bottom two rods catch just as many fish? You bet.

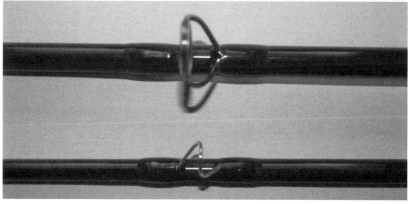

Be sure to purchase a rod with a large first and second guide, pictured on the top rod. And the remaining guides, except for the tip-top, should be snake-style guides.

What Rod Do I Really Need?

Use the following flow chart to get your answer.

1. Do you fish primarily for trout? If yes, go to number 2. If no, go to number 8.
2. Do you like to fish small creeks or bigger rivers? If bigger rivers, go to number 4.
3. You want an 8.6-foot 5-weight rod.
4. Do you live in an area where rivers tend to be more windy than not? If yes, proceed to number 5. If no, go to number 6.
5. You want a 9-foot 6-weight rod.
6. Do you expect to do any fishing from a drift boat or raft? If yes, go to number 5. If no, proceed to number 7.
7. You want a 9-foot 5-weight rod.
8. Do you fish primarily for bass, either largemouth or smallmouth? If yes, proceed to number 9. If no, go to number 10.
9. You want a 9' 7-weight rod.
10. Do you fish for carp or steelhead? If so, proceed to number 11. If no, go to number 12.
11. You want a 9-foot 7-weight rod.
12. Do you fish primarily saltwater for any of the following species: bonefish, stripers, or jacks? If yes, proceed to number 13. If no, go to question 14.
13. You want a 9-foot 8-weight rod.
14. If you are at this question you are probably not that frugal a fly fisher. Since you are here, you are targeting larger game species like permit, tarpon, and sailfish. These are not typically low-cost endeavors.

Note: See chapter 13, page 152, for more information on rods.

Chapter 4

Fly-Fishing Reels: Landing a Value Instead of Being Taken to the Cleaners

In part because of their elegant simplicity, fly-fishing reels are wonderful tools.

Pawl-and-click, disc drag, palm drag, bar stock, titanium, large arbor … Historically, a fly-fishing reel was a contraption meant solely for storing, and then paying out, fly line. Today the fly reel serves the same purpose, but modern technology is responsible for lighter and more responsive reels.

For the frugal fly fisher, a wider selection makes it harder to choose a reel. Ten years ago options for budget-minded fly fishers sacrificed quality and features. Today the frugal fly fisher has access to reels that could potentially last a lifetime, with features for most fishing situations.

A reel can be a thing of beauty or an afterthought in your gear arsenal, but its utilitarian nature cannot be understated.

Moe Witschard; moephotography.com

Both these reels have pawl-and-click drags, and both will work great for most fishing situations.

For years the most important factor in choosing a reel was its drag system—pawl-and-click or disc drag. Other systems have since come onto the market, but it's probably best to stick to what's been tested over time. Disc drag reels tend to be a little more costly, although recent advancements have made them more accessible.

Most anglers choose a disc drag because resistance is applied smoothly and across a wider range. This allows for a slower "start-up" of the drag system. The slower start-up creates a gradual application of pressure. Think of a car shifting from gears one to two and so on. A disc drag makes that transition smoother.

A pawl-and-click reel is just that—a pie-shaped pawl that pokes into the grooves on a circular click. Much like the inner workings on a watch, a pawl-and-click drag system has lots of moving parts, but the drag pressure is applied at one specific spot. The start-up speed for a pawl-and-click is more abrupt than a disc drag.

Most anglers cannot tell the difference between a pawl-and-click and a disc drag system with a fish on the line—and that is the meat of the issue. Glossy marketing and celebrity endorsements aside, the difference between the two is hard to decipher.

A disc drag with its more progressive start-up speed has a clear benefit in one specific situation—a big fish swimming away from you fast when you have low-pound test tippet. The decision on pawl-and-click versus disc drag now becomes a little trickier. A disc drag might give you a better chance of keeping the fish on rather than breaking the tippet.

Whether you choose a pawl-and-click or disc drag is a judgment call.

Lube It: At least once a season lube all the moving parts of your reels. Use "reel lube" made for fly-fishing reels. Do not use WD-40 or motor oil; should they get on your fly line, the line will be ruined in no time.

Anglers today have it easier because a few years ago disc drag reels were consistently more spendy. Today that's changed, so really the decision is entirely yours. Prioritize the realistic benefit that a given reel will add to your fishing experience.

There is a split in the fly-fishing community regarding the benefits a reel can offer. The dividing line is most noticeable between those anglers who fish in saltwater and those who fish primarily freshwater. Most saltwater anglers feel a reel is a vital piece of their arsenal, and they are correct—a

These reels have sealed disc drag mechanisms. The drag system is housed in the metal casing, protecting it from the elements.

Both of these reels will catch fish. However, the reel on the right has been catching fish for over ten years and hundreds of days and cost $30. The reel on the left cost five times that.

saltwater environment is harsh. The fish are larger and the conditions corrosive, and because many saltwater destinations are a ways from the nearest fly shop, exceptional quality and durability trumps frugality.

But most freshwater fly-fishing situations present smaller fish, easier conditions, and closer proximity to a fly shop. Naturally, the latter isn't always the case if you are backpacking in the high country or on a multiday float trip, but in general most frugal fly fishers are going to be freshwater anglers who haven't ventured too far from the nearest fly shop.

So how do you prioritize the benefits of a reel? There are several ways. Consider the species of fish you are targeting and be realistic about its average size. If you fish for trout, bass, or most warm-water species, your fishing will require a reel that is durable and effective. It doesn't need to be titanium or gold-plated or a limited edition or have a drag system powerful enough to stop a Kentucky Derby winner in its tracks, but it does need to be a system that won't fail, and it needs to be durable enough to last. Expect to spend between $35 and $150 on a reel that will last and be applicable in nearly every fishing situation. A quality reel matched to your rod will be around 50 percent of your rod cost.

Don't get caught up desiring a reel that is more than you need. Granted, each piece of water has its elusive 10-pound brown trout, 15-pound bass, or 20-pound pike, but the reality is you are going to catch a lot of smaller fish before you catch a lifetime trophy. If you do catch your personal trophy fish on a reel purchased with a budget in mind, you are going to be far enough along in your angling skills that you will be able to land the fish with ease on the less expensive reel.

Before you polish your angling skills, do some research on the reels and evaluate what you think you desire. But do so with the confidence that no matter whether you choose a disc drag or a pawl-and-click system, it isn't going to make or break your fishing.

Reels typically have two main parts: the spool and the reel itself. The spool is the circular part of the reel that holds the line. Be sure to purchase a reel that allows for the spool to be completely removed. This makes changing and detangling line a lot easier.

Spools also come in sizes of arbor. Arbor is the diameter of the spool. Ten years ago large-arbor reels were hard to come by and expensive. Today most, if not all, reel manufacturers are making large-arbor reels. There are arguments both for and against these reels. The pros: Your line lies in larger coils so it has less memory and is often easier to cast. Because it is coiled larger it can also be reeled in with fewer revolutions. But the

The reel on the left is a large arbor. The reel on the right is a small arbor. Both will work fine.

Right- or Left-Hand Retrieve: Which is the best? Whatever you prefer. The pros of right-hand retrieve: If you are right-handed, casting a lot, and catching a lot of big fish, you may want to now cast and fish all with the same arm, and you may be able to reel faster with your right hand. The pros of left-hand retrieve: You don't have to switch arms if the fish gets on the reel. It is a matter of personal preference.

cons: They can be more costly and can be heavier or feel bulkier on your rod. If cost is the determining factor, choose the less expensive option.

Notice all the extra line coming off the spool. This angler has hooked a fish. A large-arbor reel will collect this extra line faster.

The best reels are cut entirely from bar stock and contain fewer moving parts. Find one of these that fits your budget and you are good to go. An anodized reel is ideal (although most reels are anodized these days), and the internal parts (drag mechanism and shaft) should always be protected from the elements. Finally, consider if a reel can be switched easily from left-hand retrieve to right-hand retrieve, and vice versa. This is not a requirement but a nice convenience (you might loan the reel to a friend, or decide to sell it at some point).

The reels on the right have encased disc drag systems. The reels on the left are pawl-and-click reels. The pawl-and-click reels will require much more care and cleaning.

If you expect to fish more than a day or two a week, then opt for a little more durable reel with a more reliable drag system. Durability is very important if you plan to fish a lot, but also very important if you treat your gear roughly. By spending a few extra bucks you will get a reel that will last through a few more drops or dings, or an extra time you leave it on the truck topper and drive off before it's too late.

Where you fish is also a consideration. If you hike and fish mountain streams, where a slip on a rock could mean bashing or breaking your reel, consider durability, but if you fish mostly ponds or from a boat, then durability is not as crucial. Trout streams and most rivers do not require long casts; therefore, line memory is not often an issue, so a large arbor isn't essential. For lakes or ponds, or in scenarios where longer casts are optimal, a large-arbor reel will come in handy. The arbor question (whether large or small) is not written in stone; it is personal preference. Compared to ten-plus years ago, there are many manufacturers making a plethora of model options, so finding a reel that suits your budget and personal preference is not the hard part—deciphering through all the options is.

Knot Needed: In order to fish effectively, you really only need to learn three knots: a nail knot, which connects fly line to leader; a blood knot, which connects leader to tippet; and a clinch knot, which connects fly to tippet. Good knots keep you from losing gear. Losing gear costs you money.

Chapter 5

Real-Life Frugal Fly Fishers:
Michael Gracie

Name: *Michael Gracie*
Location: *Rocky Mountains*
Blog: *Michaelgracie.com*

www.michaelgracie.com

Not many shortcuts exist to become a better angler, but there are shortcuts in getting more value for your fly-fishing dollar. There are certain things a frugal fly fisher still needs to know—tips and tricks that can only be passed along from angler to angler. The anglers featured in the Real-Life Frugal Fly Fishers chapters have been in your shoes, and have walked, or

45

waded, about as far as anyone. Take their advice. Even if you do not agree with all of it, you are guaranteed to learn something new.

Michael Gracie has been around the bush a few times, but mysteriously lacks a lot of the scars to show it. Professionally, he's been involved in the world of technology and finance for his whole career. Today, he describes himself as a perpetual novice (aren't we all?) at catching fish with a fly. When not chasing tail, he can be found near his home at the foot of the Rocky Mountains scoping out the nearest watering hole or sharing his expertise of the markets. Once a self-proclaimed "gear whore," he left the dark side of hoarding behind and has developed a knack for whittling down gear to only the essentials. His lifelong passion for fly fishing benefits all frugal fly fishers.

How were you introduced to fly fishing?
The first fish I caught was a bluegill, on an old bamboo rod with a Pflueger reel, with my dad. I was around five years old, and of course there was a worm on the end. When I was around ten years old, I started fishing consistently with a neighbor friend—primarily we used baitcasters and plastic worms. He had a fly rod, and occasionally casted poppers. I thought it was too cool and saved my allowance for a year for a Shakespeare Sigma combo.

Did you learn the bulk of your fly-fishing skills from another angler or on your own? You know trial-and-error; grab-and-go; high-risk, high-reward.
I think what skill I have was actually taken from a conventional fisherman, a buddy I used to fish with in high school and occasionally still visit today. It was about finding fish—figuring out where they might be at different times of the day and year, and targeting those high-probability spots like our lives depended on it.

Who do you look to for motivation to keep at it?
When I got serious about fly-only fishing, Lefty Kreh's books were the biggest help. I could see immediate improvement from following his written instruction.

What level of angler would you rate yourself?

Pure intermediate, but with keen observation skills. I'm not shy about emulating those having more success. Luck doesn't hurt either.

Where might you suggest be the best place for cheap or free but useful instruction?

For fly tying, YouTube. For everything else, it's all about getting out there.

———

Fly fishing is a sport where gear is paramount to enjoyment. It is also very important for success, and there is a fine line between blowing your wad on gear that is beyond your ability or not a true necessity. Gear is personal—some anglers love their rods, some love their reels, some think waders are the most important item in a gear arsenal.

What one piece of gear is the most important and why?

The fly rod! You have to find a rod (or manufacturer) that suits your casting and fighting style, *and* instills confidence in you, the angler. A friend once told me when it came to the car you own, you should buy something you feel great about driving each and every day, something you are never disappointed with. That's how I feel about fly rods.

What one piece of gear is the most overrated?

Your vest, or in my case, the hip pack. I use a standard MountainSmith Tour for everything from trout to carp to bonefish, and it has never failed me. When it isn't full of fly boxes, it makes a darn good crushed beer can tote.

What do you think is a seriously overlooked piece of gear?

I don't carry a lot of gear anymore. My pack houses more snacks than fly boxes. But . . . socks are so overlooked by anglers today! You have to have good socks, as you are going to be on your feet a lot. For cold-water conditions, make sure they will keep your feet warm even when wet, as

Michael Gracie; www.michaelgracie.com

Mike has pared down his gear so that he can fish just about any piece of water in the United States using a rod, reel, and a fanny pack. Here he has shouldered his fanny pack to release a gorgeous rainbow.

most waders will eventually leak. I mean thick, soft wool socks. For warm water, I go for thin synthetic that dries fast and protects against blisters. Foot care is numero uno.

You talk some about "paring down" your gear. What do you mean by that? And how did you get to the point of knowing what you needed and what you didn't need?

Several years ago I found myself with around twenty rods. Some I barely used, while others were really only suitable for very specific situations, like heavy streamers or micro dry flies. I looked at what stick I did use the most, and for the widest variety of conditions, which one I just picked up the most regardless. Then I bought a second, used rod from the same manufacturer and quickly realized that while it was a completely differ-ent rod action it possessed most of the same characteristics that always attracted me to the former.

I wound up selling every rod I owned except those two, and then filled out my quiver with rods from that single manufacturer. I now own just seven rods and haven't felt short-changed, undergunned, or otherwise disappointed with the decision once.

After doing this for so long, I am sure you have lots of gear advice—what is one "gear epiphany" you had?
The rod racks in my SUV are Bell-brand crossbar clothes hangers I bought at AutoZone for $16. It's the best $16 I ever spent on fly-fishing related gear.

What are your top three gear-related tips to extend the life of your gear?
Wipe down your rods and reels after every outing, fresh or salt. Dirt builds up on ferrules and moving parts, scratching and wearing down as it goes.

Don't lean rods against cars. Stuff them inside the vehicle or on top of it during breaks. Otherwise, they always find their way into a door jamb.

Don't leave gear in the car 24/7. If the heat doesn't get to it and the door doesn't either, thieves eventually will.

———

For folks wanting to stretch their angling dollars or just wishing they could fish more, finding fishing close to home is crucial. Most of us are not fortunate to live ten minutes from the Madison River or on a canal near Loggerhead Basin, so the time comes when a little research needs to be done. Putting in a little time in finding locations close to home is essential to fishing frugal.

When you first started fly fishing, was it hard to find places to fish close to home?
I spent my formative years in Florida, where the concern was not finding places to fish but finding places where you didn't run into too many alligators or poisonous snakes.

Do you use modern-day tools like the Internet and/or social networking sites?

Nothing has improved my enjoyment of fly fishing more than my own blog and following the blogs of others. It has allowed me to meet people I would have never otherwise met, and frankly it's the people that make the difference.

No matter if it was hard or not, how did you find places? (Don't give away your secret places, obviously, but did you read about them somewhere or meet guys in angling clubs or just hop in the car and find water?)

I've done it all, from scouring Google Earth and uploading coordinates to my GPS, to buying people too many beers, thereby getting them to spill the beans. I never walk into a shop without asking about the latest spots either.

There is a lot of talk out there amongst veteran fly fishers about "giving up secret spots" and places being too crowded. Do you feel there are still uncrowded places to fish?

I think there is an awful lot of water out there, and whether or not it has "been discovered" very much depends on time. Has it been discovered during the rainbow or brown spawn, or at this or that flow, before or after runoff, when the water's crystal clear or tainted or flat out mud?

I doubt every possible condition, all those variables, have been tested on each and every location, and it's that very change which makes fly fishing so challenging, and ultimately satisfying, as a sport.

Do you fish for nontraditional species, such as carp or shad or another species?

My dirty little secret is I caught my first trout at twenty-six years of age. My heart has always been in the warm water, and if I lived in the Rockies for the rest of my life, I'd probably still be hard-pressed to say I caught more trout than largemouth bass. I've found some good bass spots close by, but I really had to pry them out of people.

Michael with a nice "golden ghost." Carp are gaining in popularity. They provide exciting sight-fishing opportunities close to home.

When I discovered carp, however, a lot of things changed. This last year I've trout fished in the mountains roughly ten days; meanwhile I've chased carp better than fifty days. Carp are the ultimate fly-fishing target as far as I'm concerned.

Carp? Seriously. But you've fished a lot of places, and you think carp are the ultimate target? You have to explain that statement.
First, carp are fish of leisure; i.e., they aren't always eating like trout. In other words, they have selective metabolisms. Second, their sense of vibration and smell is amazing—I've seen pods of carp spook when I'm walking by 30 feet above the bank, and watched carp turn and bolt from me standing upstream, a hundred feet away. Third, they never give up—you can have a carp in the net and they're still trying to break free. Finally, they're everywhere, which means I never have to go far to fish for them.

What is a favorite memory about discovering a new place to fish or species close to home?

A childhood friend and I found this lake just a bike ride from our neighborhood that was full of alligator gar—*big* alligator gar. We started fishing this lake every day after school, and I got in trouble for coming home after dark a few times too. We were catching gar that were upwards of 4 feet long, consistently, but nobody believed us. So one day we killed two of them and dragged them home behind our bikes. After that, everyone asked where we were going, but we kept our mouths shut. Then soccer season started, and my buddy was telling me every day at school how many he was catching while I was at practice. I wound up quitting the soccer team to fish, and nobody except the coach thought that was a bad decision.

What is the best piece of advice for anglers wanting to fish closer to home?

Be patient, as often you are treading in new territory. I think most fly fishers start the sport on trout, but when you hit urban or suburban water, it's a different game. No more gorgeous scenery, and the fish are often a lot more wary because they run into people so often.

The natural progression for a lot of fly fishers is fishing close to home and then venturing to far-off places. And by far off I mean a day's drive or more of a flight to get to the destination. A lot of the appeal is clever marketing, but a good chunk of the appeal is because Rochester, New York, or Chicago or Baltimore are not all that dandy in the middle of January. Fly fishing has the ability to open up lots of exciting travel opportunities. However, there is a fine line to walk between going broke traveling to fish and enjoying it. A bonefish may not care about your credit score, but your bank or your kids' college fund does.

Was it a long time before you invested time and money on a destination trip?

Yes. I was in my late twenties before I traveled to fish. We went to the Keys, which was already pretty familiar. We rented a dumpy duplex and a boat, and spent most of our time chasing schoolie dorado. We hit the grocery store just once, but still ate very well.

www.michaelgracie.com

Michael enjoys chasing saltwater fish. This juvenile redfish came on one of his trips when he chose to hire a guide . . . and it paid off.

Have you done any DIY (do-it-yourself) trips to far-off destinations?
I've done one completely DIY trip—it was in the Bahamas. We got skunked, badly—four days out and didn't catch one fish. We wound up drinking away our sorrows, and of course, our DIY savings.

Are these DIY itineraries something you suggest to frugal fly fishers if they have never been to a destination before?
If they have some experience targeting the species, then it's just luck of the draw. If it's, say, your first time bonefishing or redfishing, I think you are wasting money by *not* hiring a guide, so absolutely hire a guide proficient at the species—you've got a good chance of having fun and saving money.

When you travel to fish what are some bits of advice you would pass along?
Travel as light as possible, but not so light that once you break a piece of equipment or lose a fly that your trip is finished. I'm not big on fancy

Michael with one of his lifelong fly-fishing heroes—Lefty Kreh.

luggage either; I think it attracts attention. I use old duffle bags with no labels on them, and carry rods, reels, and flies with me whenever possible. Carry travelers checks and only cash them when you are dead broke. You'll be surprised at how much less you spend on the frivolous when you don't have currency on you. Lastly, pack some favorite, nonperishable snacks in your checked luggage.

For those anglers willing to hire a guide, any words of advice?
References, references, references! Try fishing with guides who you've heard about through friends. There's too much communication swirling around for anyone to have to fish with a random name out of the Yellow Pages, and the fly-fishing world is a pretty small one to boot.

We've already talked about gear. Are there other things frugal fly fishers can do to save some cash and still experience great fly fishing?
Network, network, network! I rarely fish alone, mostly because I usually enjoy the company and conversation as much as the fishing. Meeting fellow fly fishers through seminars, happy hours, fly-tying sessions, or

online social networks means you'll always have someone you can share the experiences with. And share the gas money with.

What would be your favorite books or websites for tips and techniques?
As for books, I really like *Practical Fishing Knots* by Mark Sosin and Lefty Kreh. *Longer Fly Casting* by Kreh and *The Little Red Book of Fly Fishing* by Charlie Meyers and Kirk Deeter. For websites I like MidCurrent.com and *Field and Stream*'s FlyTalk.com.

Any last words of advice?
Yeah, don't even try learning anything from that michaelgracie.com site— it's 100 percent bullshit!

Chapter 6

Fly Line: The Straight and Narrow on a Necessity

Frugal fly fishers certainly don't buy the most expensive rods or the shiniest reels. Their waders are patched with duct tape and superglue, and their lucky felt hats were new during one of the big wars. However, the smartest cheapskates always have top-quality fly lines. A high-end fly line will upgrade any rod it is fished with and, if cared for, will last considerably longer than a lesser-quality fly line. The better quality, and often more expensive, fly lines have a more durable finish, the manufacturers often add slicker lubricants to that finish, and the core of the fly line is of stronger materials.

The number of options for fly lines has exploded in recent years. From shooting heads to depth charge sink-tips to "slime lines" to nymph tapers, it seems like anglers have as many choices in fly lines as they do in flies. And like fly selection, choosing a fly line is important for success and enjoyment. Your investment in better fly line will only cost you about $50 more than the cheap route.

If it's been awhile since your fly line last saw the light of day, take a few minutes to stretch out the memory. Fly line coils become progressively tighter the longer they sit on the reel.

Fly lines, like rods, are weighted from a scale of 0 to 14, with 0 being the thinnest and 14 being the thickest. In general line weights 0 to 3 are used primarily for small creeks and rivers that contain trout, and small ponds or backwaters that contain panfish or perch or smaller species.

Line weights 4 and 5 are fished in a variety of environments, including larger rivers and lakes and ponds. A 5-weight is perhaps the best

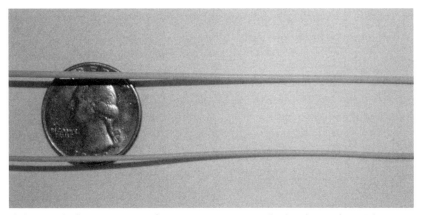

Fly lines gradually increase in size from 0 to 14. Here are a 6- (top) and 5-weight, weight-forward, floating lines.

all-around line weight. Line weights of 6 and 7 work fine for trout and bass but might be overkill for a few trout fishing situations, particularly trout in small creeks. For big bass, a 6-weight might be too small, but a 7-weight should handle most any bass flies *and* big bass. These line weights are also ideal for most steelhead unless you tap into a lifetime trophy. Line weights 6 and 7 can also work well for redfish and sea trout.

Once you pass 7-weight, you are into lines that will most likely be fished in saltwater. Some steelhead streams are best fished with a line weight of 8, but more anglers are fishing steelhead rivers with a line weight of 7. With line weights 8 and 9, the primary targets will

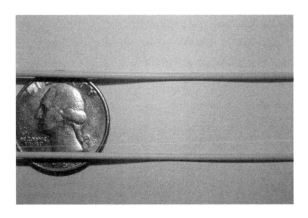

You can see the subtle difference between a 10-weight (top) and a 9-weight. Many anglers choose to over-line their rods, so if they have a 9-weight rod they will use a 10-weight. This makes the rod easier to load when casting.

be redfish, bonefish, permit, and the occasional tarpon. Once you get above line weights 9 and 10, large saltwater gamefish are the primary target—100+ pound tarpon, giant trevally, sailfish, and a few other species are the focus.

Fly lines, regardless of weight, range from floating to full sinking to intermediate sinking and more. For most trout fishing situations a floating line will work. For most saltwater situations a floating line will also do the trick. If you plan to fish mostly ponds or lakes for bass or other warmwater species, a floating line will work about half the time, but you may also want to consider a sinking or sink-tip line. If you require different lines, consider buying a reel and owning multiple spools in the reel model. Load the extra spools with various types of fly lines.

When loading a new line onto a reel, be sure to tag it with a permanent marker so you know its type, weight, and whether it floats or sinks. For example; WF-5-F. That's a Weight Forward, 5-Weight, Floating line.

Floating fly lines come in a few styles: weight-forward, double taper, level taper, and a shooting taper. A weight-forward taper is a little easier to cast as the weight of the fly line is at the front end of the line, allowing for more energy efficiency during your cast. A double taper fly line has an even taper at both ends of the line, so after a year or so you could reverse which end of the fly line is attached to your backing and have, in essence, a new fly line. A level taper is just that—a line that has no taper; it is the same diameter for the length of the line. A shooting taper has a heavily weighted front taper, even heavier than most weight-forwards, and then a long and thin amount of fly line. Shooting tapers are good for long casts when mending or a lot of line management isn't required, but they're also very specialized lines, and so not necessary for most frugal fly fishermen.

Double taper lines are better for short casts and for casts that require a softer or more delicate presentation of leader and fly. If you fish mostly small creeks, then a double taper might be the best option; otherwise go

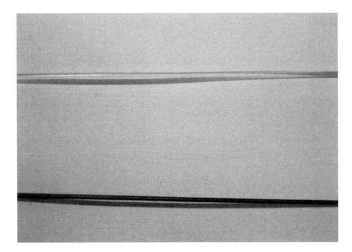

There are many sinking-type lines available. The top line is a clear sinking line. The bottom is a sink-tip line.

with a weight forward as its ability to cast farther and manage line a little easier will make your fishing more enjoyable.

Fly lines are coded, or labeled, based on their line weight and the type of taper, whether weight forward or double taper. For example, a weight-forward floating fly line with a line weight of 5 is labeled WF-5-F. Translation: weight forward, 5, floating. A double taper floating fly line with a line weight of 6 is labeled DT-6-F. If any confusion still lingers, there is often a description on the box.

Most frugal fly fishers pursuing trout will want a line that is weight forward or a double taper in a 5-weight. If larger rivers or ponds are going to be fished more often than small rivers, a 6-weight might be considered, but many times that will be a little large. If bass on ponds and larger rivers is the target species, then a weight forward 6- or 7-weight line is ideal.

As for sinking and sink-tip lines, they are often used in very specific fishing situations. For many years, trout anglers only used them when fishing lakes or ponds. Even saltwater flats anglers rarely used sinking or sink-tip fly lines. Bass and steelhead anglers often used them because the nature of their fishing required flies to be submerged quickly. In the past ten years more trout anglers on larger rivers have been using sink-tip lines. And many saltwater anglers, especially when pursuing tarpon, have been using sink-tip lines or full sinking lines.

No Wilty Lines: If fishing saltwater, be sure to research your fly line before making your first cast. Many freshwater lines lack the stiffness to cast effectively in warmer waters.

This doesn't mean a frugal fly fisher should ignore sink-tip or full sinking lines, but the bulk of your fly line budget should be spent on a high-quality floating fly line. If you still desire a sink-tip, fly line manufacturers have created quick-attaching sink-tips that can be tied onto any fly line via a loop-to-loop connection, eliminating the need for a separate sink-tip fly line and reel to hold it.

After investing a proportionally larger chunk of cash on your fly line, be sure to buy a few vials of line dressing or cleaner. Carry a vial with you or put it in your vest or pack and be sure to use it. The easiest way to ensure your fly line lasts as long as you intended is constantly keeping your lines clean. Devoting five minutes to your line after each outing can lengthen its life span line by several seasons.

If your reel did not come with a reel case, consider purchasing one, if only to protect your line. Most fishing vests or packs collect tiny bits of sand and gravel. If your fly line is not protected in your reel case, the grit and grime will find its way to your line.

Choosing the right fly line and caring for it is not as easy as it sounds. Choosing the right fly line means you still have to sift through all of the new gear. For frugal fly fishers you have to take the good with the bad. Once you've sifted through all the options you will come out with a fly line that, when treated with care, will give you a great bang for your buck.

Chapter 7

Flies: A Little Knowledge Goes a Long Way

Experienced anglers often claim that a fish doesn't care how much you paid for your fly rod, reel, or even flies. True enough, but learning how to use the proper flies is crucial—no matter how much money you want to spend. If you thought the options for rods, reels, and fly lines were numerous, then prepare to be amazed at your local fly shop because the hundreds of flies in various patterns and sizes is sure to blow your mind.

By this point in your quest to fish frugal, you've done a respectable job keeping your costs down. But the reality is you have to invest money or time into choosing, and fishing, the right fly at the right time. You also

Big dry flies are the pinnacle of fishing for many trout anglers—this fish made a bad choice.

The fly selection at your local fly shop will rival, and beat, any big-box store hands-down.

must decide between finding time to learn to tie flies or spending that time doing something else—like being with family or friends or that annoying little habit called work.

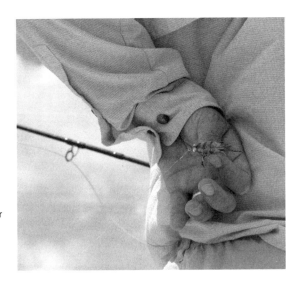

Whether you tie or buy your flies, choosing the right fly can mean the difference between hooking up and waiting for action.

From the JP Special to the WD-40 to the Little Green Machine to the Royal Wulff, innovation in flies is responsible for the explosion in fly pattern options. The use of artificial materials, cheap labor on the international market, and the proven success of new patterns a-stream or a-flat are responsible for the ever-increasing size of the fly bin at the fly shop. As enticing as it may seem to want the newest and hottest fly patterns, the frugal fly fisher has a tough decision to make. Do I invest in new flies, or do I invest in educating myself in fly tying? Or some combination thereof?

A carpenter is not going to spend hours, or dollars, choosing the best tools only to go out and buy crappy nails or poor screws. The same is true for choosing the right fly or tying the right flies.

This chart quantifies, as best as possible, the costs of buying flies versus tying flies. It takes time to learn to tie flies well. No time is required to pick out and pay for flies. You have to decide how important

Tying Flies

Fly-tying kit, including vise, assorted materials	$100
Time it takes to learn to effectively tie a dozen fly patterns	40 hours
Acquiring and maintaining materials	$100
Satisfaction of tying your own flies	Your price
Average number of flies necessary to fish	50
Average cost to tie your flies—not counting your time	$200
Average cost to tie your flies PLUS your time	$200 + Your time

Buying Flies

Average cost of flies purchased from an online outlet	$10/dozen
Average cost of flies purchased from fly shop	$15/dozen
Time saved in letting someone else tie	Your price
Average number of flies necessary to fish	50
Average cost to buy your flies—a mix of online and store-bought	$625

When waters get dirty with mud or silt, fish a bigger fly and one with more flash. Size is often more important than color, but play around till you find a color to match the increased turbidity of the water.

the intrinsic value of tying flies *and* catching fish on flies you tied is versus just catching fish on any fly. The decision is yours. No one can make it for you.

Sifting through thousands of different flies can be fun, but not practical. Spending hours at a vise learning to tie is enjoyable for some and cost-effective because raw materials are relatively cheap, but the time spent tying and learning to tie may outweigh the precious spare time you have.

The decision to buy or tie your flies is entirely up to you. The long-term frugal solution will always be tying your own flies. There is no arguing that statement.

Buying flies is a shortcut. In the past, buying flies online or from a wholesale distributor was a dicey option—quality was always a

For the price of all the flies on the left you can buy all the materials on the right and tie ten times the flies.

mystery. Today, there are several fly distributors who sell to the general public.

Locally, or when you are traveling to a far-off destination, a local fly shop is going to be your best bet for proven flies on local waters. Sure, you can save a dollar a fly by purchasing online, but those flies may not catch fish on local or far-off waters. Despite what your pocketbook thinks, local knowledge trumps saving money nine times out of ten.

Most fly shops are enjoyable places to spend time. They are staffed by friendly and informative employees. The have the latest trends in gear. They offer up-to-the-minute information. They want your business and they also want to make your experience as enjoyable and efficient as possible. So why do their fly and fly-tying selections change year-in and year-out? Are the trout really not eating the same flies they were ten years ago? Do you really need the latest in fly patterns, or will the flies your father fished suffice? The answer, unfortunately for the frugal angler, is "yes and no."

Selecting the right fly might be the single most important decision in fly fishing. At the risk of oversimplifying fly fishing, the fly is what the fish see. Not your tight loops or your airplane-grade, bar-stock, artistic reel. Granted, you can't get the fly where it needs to be without a rod and reel and fly line, but you are not going to eat that cheeseburger at Hooters if the bun looks moldy and the meat is raw no matter how little clothing the waitresses wear. Investing time into understanding why fish choose a fly and what makes a fly successful is the frugal decision—not buying a fly because it looks good or it's the "hot" fly.

Presentation of your fly is more important than choosing the perfect fly. The idea of presentation is a broad concept. For the purpose of sorting through the abundance of flies to keep a little extra cash in your

A Little Twitch: If fishing a fly that is supposed to move—a caddis, a hopper, a saltwater crab or baitfish—don't be afraid to get a little twitchy with it. When placing your cast, take into account that you are going to twitch the fly, so don't over- or under-aim your cast too much.

A basic understanding of insects and baitfish is important to any angler's success.

Andy Sabota: www.Midwestflyworks.com

pocket, presentation in this chapter will stick to how the fly looks to the fish—things like getting a drag-free drift and reading water are essential to becoming a better angler, but they are not essential in getting the most bang for your buck when selecting your flies.

Flies for trout fishing fit into a few categories. The most often used are dry flies, nymphs, and streamers. Two other categories exist—emergers and Soft-Hackles—but most trout can be caught on a dry, nymph, or streamer regardless of fishing conditions or time of year. The interesting aspect of fishing emergers and Soft-Hackles, despite their relative lack of use, is that fishing emergers is a new concept in fly fishing, but fishing Soft-Hackles is a more time-tested method. Both styles of fly catch fish when fished well and at a very specific time, but in selecting your flies with your pocketbook in mind, you can ignore the two.

Before choosing flies it is important you know the difference between nymphs, drys, and streamers. Nymphs and streamers are flies that sink and imitate food under the surface or on the bottom of the river. Dry flies imitate food on the surface of the water. Most dry flies are fished floating on the surface of the water and can be seen by the angler. A dry fly floating on the surface of a trout stream is the adult stage of most aquatic insects' life cycles.

If you are matching a hatch and you get a refusal, clip your fly's hackle or wing a tad, or use a black marker to darken the body. Sometimes just a little change does the trick.

Trout eat aquatic insects more than anything else. They also eat the occasional terrestrial insect, for example, grasshoppers, ants, and beetles. Trout also eat other trout and small baitfish. Nymphs and dry flies imitate insects while streamers most often imitate other trout or small baitfish.

Fourteen Essential Patterns and Their Sizes for Trout Fishing

Nymphs

Beadhead Prince sizes 10 and 14
Beadhead Pheasant Tail sizes 16 and 18
Beadhead Zebra Midge sizes 18 and 20
Beadhead caddis pupa sizes 12 and 14
Beadhead orange scud size 12

Dry Flies

Olive Elk Hair Caddis sizes 12 and 16
Royal Stimulator sizes 6 and 10
Parachute Adams sizes 14 and 18
Tan Chubby Chernobyl sizes 6 and 10
Purple Haze sizes 10 and 16
Harrop's Hairwing Dunn sizes 14 and 16

Streamers

Olive Wooly Bugger sizes 4 and 8
Muddler Minnow size 4
Trick-or-Treat sizes 4 and 6

> Don't give up on a drift until you've let the fly swing across and up in the water. Trout chase emerging insects, so keep your fly in the water as much as possible. Many flies can be fished as both a dry and a wet fly.

Every trout fisher's fly box should contain a selection of nymphs, drys, and streamers. The flies that you carry ultimately depend on where you do most of your fishing. If you fish larger rivers more than smaller creeks, your fly selection will be different than if you fish rivers that are crystal clear and are spring creeks or tailwaters. If you fish a wide array of waters, then your selection will need further refinement.

Most trout rivers are home to mayflies, caddis, and stoneflies. If you find yourself on spring creeks or tailwater rivers, trout will be eating midges, freshwater shrimp, and a few other aquatic insects. Mayflies, caddis, stoneflies, and midges all have adult stages of their life cycle, which means you will encounter fish eating dry flies on the surface. On any given day of trout fishing on any given river, a trout may feed on nymphs and then switch to feeding on dry flies. It is also possible the trout may be pursuing baitfish. Deciphering a trout's feeding habits and then fishing the right fly in the proper manner are skills that take a lifetime to master . . . but you can always try a few shortcuts.

Most saltwater gamefish from Maine to Mexico and around to Baja eat baitfish. Understanding the life cycle of insects is not important at all. Finding feeding fish is paramount in most saltwater angling situations—and that requires intimate knowledge of tides, flats, currents, and minor changes in depth. Whether you are pursuing permit, tarpon, bonefish, bluefish, stripers, or roosterfish, you can keep your fly selection to around a dozen patterns.

Fly selection for saltwater angling is more about action in the water than size or color. Saltwater gamefish are predators, so your fly must imitate its prey. Most successful saltwater patterns have a few key elements: oversize eyes, an elongated shape to imitate a baitfish or minnow, and a variation in color to imitate the lateral line of a baitfish.

Essential Patterns for Saltwater Fly Fishing

Size is going to be relative to the species you are fishing for. With the exception of the Tarpon Toad, when choosing size, pick one that is relative to the depth of water and the size of the species you're fishing for. Shallow depth, smaller fly; bigger fish, bigger fly.

Chartreuse Deep Clouser minnow
Chartreuse lightly weighted Clouser minnow
Tan or gray Silly Legs Gotcha
Lefty's Deceiver
A weighted version of any crab
An un-weighted of any crab

Many of us fish saltwater as a luxury—when the trout rivers of our home waters are under snow and we desire warmer climes. Because air travel is required for most saltwater destinations, unless you are lucky enough to live in the Florida Keys or near Baja, or fish along the Atlantic coast, saltwater fly fishing tends to be less frugal than freshwater.

Travel, boat expenses, and moderately specialized gear gravitates most saltwater experiences away from frugal. Few things fire adrenaline to the brain like the incomparable pull of a tarpon's first run or the black tail of a permit breaking the morning quiet on a saltwater flat. Saltwater fly fishing, particularly stalking permit, tarpon, or bonefish, is an experience every frugal angler should budget for and experience at least once.

Understanding that not everyone lives near a trout stream or a saltwater flat, the nearest fly-fishing opportunities may be a local pond or small creek. These smaller and lesser known bodies of water may certainly be worthy of your fly—just which fly for *which* species is the question. From Massachusetts to Montana, from Charlotte to Portland, most any body of water will hold something that will eat a fly. As long as you are willing to get out, cast a fly, and be happy with whatever hits the end of your line, fishing opportunities exist much closer than you think. And fly selection doesn't need to be a mystery or expensive either.

Top Five Flies for Any Body of Freshwater in the USA

These five patterns will imitate any food for any species of fish in any body of water in the country. Armed with these flies, the frugal angler stands the chance to catch a fish close to home.

Black, olive, or brown Wooly Bugger sizes 4 and 10
Chubby Chernobyl size 8
Beadhead Prince size 10
Clouser minnow, weighted or un-weighted size 2
Royal Wulff size 14

Trout, large- and smallmouth bass, crappie, bluegill, perch, carp, and many other species of fish swim in an abundance of waters. The excuses of not knowing which fly to use or where to fish can no longer be used. The very nature of being a frugal fly fisher is rooted in seeking out new fly-fishing opportunities close to home. So get out there and go fishing.

Andy Sabota; www.Midwestflyworks.com

This bass fell for a violently stripped popping bug.

Chapter 8

Get 'Er Done: Finding Instruction for Cheap

Learning to fly fish is a long-term commitment. This is what makes the sport so appealing—the more you do it, the more you discover how much more there is to learn. The variables of fly fishing are limitless, so there is always room to improve your skills. Wind, river currents, varying degrees of light, and the habits of fish all create obstacles to overcome.

For a beginner, it's easy to look at the amount of gear needed, the knots you have to learn, the specific casts you have to know, the appropriate behavior on the water, and become intimidated. As fly-fishing guides and outfitters prefer, you could invest a lot of money in high-quality instruction. Investing in an outfitter or guide will certainly speed up the learning process, but for a frugal fly fisher, this honestly probably isn't the best place to put your money.

Only a few years ago anyone interested in fly fishing struggled with finding instruction. If skills were not

No one knows what is happening on nearby waters better than your local fly shop. Keep your business in your neighborhood and they will reward you with up-to-date, accurate, and friendly advice.

Add up the amount of free information given away at a fly shop and it's a miracle any given shop can stay in business.

passed down by an older generation, anglers new to fly fishing relied heavily on a few quality books as well as the school of trial-and-error. The benefits of paying a little more in sweat equity to become a better angler are obvious. Self-discovery leads to self-confidence. But the good comes with the bad—need help with that nasty tailing loop or trying to get better at reading water? You have to find a friend or relative or buy a book or video.

The Internet

There is certainly a time and place for improving your skills on your own, but if you are like most people, your leisure time is more precious than you care to acknowledge. As technology aids our lives, there is also some blame to place on it in speeding-up and cluttering our daily routines. But technology can also aid you in your frugality. The Internet is free and can offer help with your double haul in less than thirty seconds. A Google search of "fly fishing instruction" returned over five million hits. "Learn to fly cast" returned over 300,000. "Learning the double haul" returned over 100,000. Granted, it is the Internet, so the bulk of these results can be dismissed as junk. But even a small percentage of 300,000 is a high number. Spend some time on the information superhighway and you will find countless resources to better your angling. From bulletin boards to YouTube video links, nearly every subject has an article or, even better, a video link.

Hints and Tips for Better Internet Searching

- Always preface any search with "fly fishing . . ." For example, if you want to become better at learning to read the water for trout, search "fly fishing reading the water" instead of "reading water." Another example: "fly fishing fixing a tailing loop."

- When watching a video link, be sure to take notes. A stream is no place for a laptop. Technology is great, but downloading videos streamside is going to be frowned upon.

- A lot of instruction is in the form of blogs. You may have to decipher through a lot of "fluff." For example, I-am-Stan-the-fly-dude-from-Andover-and-I-love-big-trout-and-big-cheeseburgers-and-the-New-York-Yankees-and-my-daughter-loves-piano-and-Dora-the-Explorer . . . you get the idea. Sift through much of the extraneous information and you can get some great stuff, but it may take some speed-reading skills or some patience.

- Old threads or comments from bulletin boards will pop up in search results. If you are not aware already, browsing on the Internet can suck up time before you know it. Do not waste time searching out threads or comments on bulletin boards if what you want is not readily available. A good general rule is five clicks. After five clicks from your initial search if you have not yet found clear and concise information, then you are wasting precious time and have crossed over into "just browsing."

- It took several years, but the major fly-fishing magazines have online editions. They offer a good resource, but there are countless independent online outlets for instruction and

73

information. Here are a few favorites: www.midcurrent.com; www.sexyloops.com; flyanglersonline.com; www.troutunder ground.com; www.406andfly.com; www.fedflyfishers.org

- Keep things in perspective. The instruction you are getting and the experience getting it have the potential to be worth the price you paid for it—free. There are some great resources online, and there is some painfully poor information out there as well. Take what is useful and use it; don't fret over something that is not. Poor-quality video downloads and sites that load slow or are hard to navigate are not worth your time.

- Don't bypass the written word. Video links are intriguing and quicker means to an end, but reading something can have a longer lasting affect.

Fly Shops

The Internet makes it easier for fly fishers to exchange information and ideas. From learning what is hatching on any given river at any time or needing help with tying a Clouser minnow, it is a bona fide goldmine of information. But if you are looking for a long-term mutually beneficial relationship, your local fly shop is going to trump the Internet. Downloading a link from Captain Joe 2,000 miles away is going to offer some help. Walking into your local dealer, fly rod in hand, armed with questions is another thing entirely. They have your best interests at heart—the better angler you become, the more you are going to enjoy fishing, thus the more coin you are going to drop in the shop.

Most fly shops are thrilled to offer advice and information. Most shop staff are happy to take ten minutes to work with you on your double haul. They are happy to get out of the shop for a bit, but also want you to learn more. Offering advice on flies and where to fish is a given in most fly shops, and every frugal fly fisher should take advantage of up-to-date and local information.

Along with free information, most shops offer classes or group instruction. These are great venues for learning without breaking your bank. What a lot of anglers find useful about a class compared to a guided trip or a weeklong guided trip is the time frame. A class often covers a few months. At the beginning of the class your skills are certainly going to be different than at the end of the class. But space a five-session class (five meetings over several months) over a fishing season, and by the middle of the class you've been able to fish some on your own—having some success but also having some new issues arise. The class environment allows for your improvement over time and the ability to target new issues as well. Plus being in an environment with fellow anglers is a good thing. Some of the best learning comes from talking with fellow anglers. Which is more conducive to learning: downloading a grainy webcast or sitting around a table drinking coffee with fellow anglers?

> Curveballs: Understand your learning curve. Look for minor bits of positive reinforcement. A well-tied knot. A fish on a size 20 dry fly. Spotting your first bonefish. If this sport were easy, everyone would do it and we'd all get bored fast.

Clubs and Groups

Local angling clubs or conservation groups can serve a dual role for the frugal fly fisher: instruction and social networking. The largest and most recognized organization is the Federation of Fly Fishers (FFF). With chapters and members in the United States and abroad, becoming a member is crucial to frugal angling. Local chapters abound and odds are good there is a chapter within two hours of your hometown. By joining a local chapter of the FFF, you get access to fellow anglers, classes, forums, auctions, and other fly-fishing related events. If this sounds like an advertisement for the FFF, well, it is—frugal fly fishers should not overlook joining a local chapter. Many local chapters bring in well-known instructors and authors for classes or presentations. If you can't figure out why your cast keeps piling in front of you, then join a local chapter of the FFF, and when Lefty Kreh comes to speak perhaps he can help you.

A great benefit of joining the FFF is the networking you will enjoy. Because the organization has been around for years, a wide array of abilities and interest abound. You will certainly find some angling companions and anglers willing to offer instruction.

For more information visit their website at www.fedflyfishers.org. If there is one organization for a frugal fly fisher to join and remain active in, the FFF is it.

Conservation groups like Trout Unlimited (TU), the Coastal Conservation Association (CCA), the Bonefish and Tarpon Trust (BTT), and others are worth pursuing membership. Most of these groups, if not all, have local chapters. In addition to doing a good deed to preserve future fisheries for the next generation of frugal fly fishers, you will be meeting and joining local anglers.

All of these organizations have monthly meetings on a local level. During these meetings they bring in speakers or host programs. The subject matter often runs the spectrum, from international destinations to casting instruction. Most organizations also offer classes at a reduced cost, and often free, to members.

Another great benefit to joining a local conservation organization is access to their auctions for raising funds. At these auctions you can get some screaming deals on gear, trips, or instructions, and your money goes to benefit conservation in your area. A win-win for all. And while at an auction, sipping a cocktail or dining at a table with a fellow member, you might learn of a new place to fish close to home.

Think National, Learn Locally: National and Regional Conservation Groups and Organizations

- Federation of Fly Fishers (FFF). Conserving, restoring, and educating through fly fishing. One of the oldest fly-fishing organizations in the world. They have local chapters throughout the United States and the world. They offer instruction and education for all levels of anglers. They are the only "fly fishing only" national organization dedicated solely to advancing the sport of fly fishing. A few regions of the FFF have created more regionally focused chapters, for example the Southern Council, Western Rocky Mountain Council, and the Mid-Atlantic Council; www.fedflyfishers.org; (406) 222-9369.

- Trout Unlimited (TU). Conserving, protecting, and restoring North America's coldwater fisheries and their watersheds. TU is a national organization, but focused a lot on the grassroots, local level. With around 400 local chapters in North America, there is sure to be a TU chapter near you; www.tu.org; (800) 834-2419.

- Coastal Conservation Association (CCA). Since 1984 the CCA has been dedicated to the conservation and restoration of coastal marine resources. Seventeen state chapters span the Gulf of Mexico, Pacific, and the Atlantic. Each state chapter is divided into smaller regional chapters. These regional chapters are the place for local angling events, instruction, and conservation; www.joincca.org; (800) 201-FISH.

- Bonefish and Tarpon Trust (BTT). A youngster among fish conservation organizations, the BTT (formerly known as Bonefish and Tarpon Unlimited) is committed to understanding and conserving bonefish and tarpon throughout the world; www.tarbone.org; (239) 283-1622.

- Atlantic Salmon Federation (ASF). Dedicated to conserving, protecting, and restoring of wild Atlantic salmon and the ecosystems the fish depend on for survival. Wild Atlantic salmon numbers went from 1.8 million in 1978 to 418,000 in 2001. It is clear their task is monumental—joining your local chapter does considerable good, and you will be surprised how many urban areas could be home to Atlantic salmon fisheries; www .asf.org; (506) 529-4581.

- Recreational Boating & Fishing Foundation (RBFF). The organization behind the national ad campaign Take Me Fishing .org, the RBFF's website of the same name is a great resource for information. They also are the founders of the Anglers' Legacy—an organization devoted to introducing new anglers to fishing; www.takemefishing.org; (703) 519-0013.

- The Nature Conservancy. Normally a conservation-only organization wouldn't be listed in a fly-fishing book. However, because The Nature Conservancy manages preserves and conservation properties throughout the United States and often allows and utilizes fishing as a means of wildlife management, they are listed. They also have state and local chapters that are useful resources; www.nature.org; (703) 841-5300.

- International Game Fish Association (IGFA). Once housed in the American Museum of Natural History, the IGFA is now recognized as a global leader in fisheries research, management, and conservation. Although they do not operate regional chapters, the IGFA is a good resource for education and general information; www.igfa.org; (954) 927-2628.

- International Women Fly Fishers (IWFF). Beginning in 1996, the organization has grown to around 250 members and expanding. The IWFF has a random assortment of local clubs throughout the United States. They are committed to connecting women interested in fly fishing with other interested women. Education, travel, and conservation are founding ideals; www.intlwomenflyfishers.org.

Books

A club is a bona fide source of information. The Internet is another great resource for instruction. However, it is not always practical to carry along a laptop to the stream; besides dropping your laptop or smartphone in the water is far more stressful than dropping a book. The pros of using books for practical, hands-on instruction are obvious—books transport easier and they handle the elements better. As quick as the gratification is upon searching the Internet, the patience required in using a book is fitting for fly fishing. There is also a historical connection between fly fishing and writing. Because the seasonal nature of fly fishing lends itself to long periods of the year when fishing is not an option, or at least less desirable than sitting by the fire, fly-fishing books allow anglers some respite.

Don't spend all your money early in your fly-fishing endeavor—save some to treat yourself to a new rod or a destination trip so you can appreciate them when you are a competent angler.

There are a few DVDs on the market today that offer good instruction as well. As the Internet and Internet-based technologies like streaming videos to a television gain in popularity and access, DVDs may become obsolete, but for now they offer great instruction for a reasonable price.

Because fly-fishing books and DVDs can be broken down into a few categories, the reviews are categorical: instructional, species or type specific (for example trout or saltwater angling), and expert instructional.

Instructional

The Curtis Creek Manifesto, **Sheridan Anderson.**

What began as fifteen pages of a unique writer's vision has become one of the most respected and well-used instructional books on fly fishing *ever*. First published in 1978, the book idea was the vision of a rugged, yet laid-back rock-climber-turned-angler-turned hippie-turned-poet. Anderson was known for tossing conventions aside and venturing into the mountains for weeks on end. Why is this important? Because it is otherwise hard to imagine a book so practical yet so unorthodox.

Domestic Tranquility: Even pros don't try to teach wives, husbands, or significant others to fly fish. Why should you? Invest money into instruction, not marriage counseling. Hire it out. Money spent will be money saved in the long term.

Illustrated and written in an informative and humorous style, the *Manifesto* is the fly-fishing instructional book that has it all. The book lacks the pretentiousness that so many other books have—there is not a chapter on chasing great species abroad, nor any chapters on the sounds or manners of fly fishing, and certainly no chapter on my great life spent fly fishing.

For fly fishers who came to the sport pre–Redford's *A River Runs Through It*, the *Manifesto* was partly responsible for bringing, and keeping, anglers involved in fly fishing. As a restorative to Brad Pitt's "shadow casting," the *Manifesto* offered a no-fluff instructional reference.

If there is still doubt that this forty-eight-page book is the greatest instructional manual, the numbers do not lie—since 1978 it has sold over 250,000 copies. Most fly-fishing books are considered big sellers if they sell 5,000. All from a writer who referred to himself as "the foe of the work ethic."

Lefty Kreh's Ultimate Guide to Fly Fishing, Lefty Kreh.

If Sheridan Anderson was the anti-hardcore angler, Lefty Kreh was the original hard-working angler and writer. Kreh is often acknowledged as the father of fly-fishing instruction. If there is an aspect of fly fishing that hasn't been written about by Lefty, then it is truly a pioneering facet of the sport. Despite his relative Elvis-like stature among fly fishers, Lefty's instruction, in person and in his books, is honest, always trimmed with good humor, and always helpful. Over the years Lefty has remained an easygoing and very approachable figure in the sport.

Lefty's Got It: It's simple—get your hands on anything Lefty Kreh authored and read it. Then read it again with a rod in your hand. Many of his books have made the rounds, so look in used bookstores or online.

Kreh's *Ultimate Guide to Fly Fishing* is the collection of the many books in his "Lefty's Little Library" series. This guide is over 420 pages of information—a stark contrast to *The Curtis Creek Manifesto*. If assembling a library of fly-fishing books is not in your budget, Kreh's book is a necessity. From rod selection for fresh and saltwater fly fishing to advanced casting techniques to fly design and selection, this guide is a reference you will return to often. There are also chapters on techniques for trout, salmon, bass, panfish, stripers, bluefish, shark, tarpon, and more species; fly-fishing rivers, lakes, inshore waters, mangroves, and more.

Kreh's *Ultimate Guide* lives up to its name, and every frugal fly fisher should have at least one book by Lefty in his or her personal library.

Species Specific
The Dry Fly: New Angles, **Gary LaFontaine.**
From his home near the Clark Fork River in Montana, Gary LaFontaine lived and breathed fly fishing. Thousands of anglers have become better fly fishers because of the time LaFontaine spent a-stream. Known for abstract and nontraditional research techniques like snorkeling or using night-vision glasses, he studied trout and insects on a regular basis.

He is the author of several useful and informative books including *Caddisflies, Mayflies, Trout Flies: Proven Patterns. The Dry Fly* is most important for frugal fly fishers because of the scope of the material.

Although the subject matter is advanced enough to fall into the expert category, the book is essential for beginning anglers because of LaFontaine's philosophical approach to trout and their feeding habits. The book has a lot of science-based observation, but it is essential in helping you choose the right fly at the right time.

Fly Fishing for Bonefish, **New and Revised, Dick Brown.**
The bonefish is built for speed. Catching a bonefish on a fly is no easy task because the saltwater flats environment doesn't lend itself to easy-peasy angling. Tides, wind, minor depth changes, and the sheer size of their environment serve up dynamic elements to challenge the angler. Except for the guides and intrepid anglers who fished the flats on a regular basis, before this book hit the shelves the flats environment remained a mystery to most anglers.

Fly Fishing for Bonefish is almost four hundred pages of flats fishing knowledge. The book's focus is on bonefish, but the information regarding tides, fly selection, setting your drag, casting, stripping techniques, stalking, tailing, and cruising fish, can apply to flats fishing for redfish, permit, and any other species that swims in shallow waters. There is even a chapter on the world's bonefishing destinations should you get the itch and it fits your angling budget!

Fly Fishing in Saltwater, 3rd Edition, Lefty Kreh.

First published twenty years ago, this book was the compendium of saltwater fly fishing. Written by Lefty Kreh, the most prolific fly-fishing writer of our time, this "bible" covers it all, from knots to species to flies to boats.

Revised and expanded, the content is updated for today's saltwater angler. With over 340 pages of text, photographs, drawings, and charts, *Fly Fishing in Saltwater, 3rd Edition* is certain to make you a better angler.

The LL Bean Fly Fishing for Bass Handbook, Dave Whitlock.

Still a relative afterthought among most fly fishers, fly fishing for bass is exciting, challenging, and worth trying. Most of the U.S. population lives closer to waters home to bass than to a trout stream.

Expert angler and talented writer Dave Whitlock covers all facets of fly fishing for bass. With chapters on the different bass species and their habitats, techniques, flies, gear, and the difference between fishing lakes and fishing streams, this is a must-have for anyone who has even toyed with the idea of fly fishing for bass. Get the book and head out . . . bass fishing is a hoot.

The Orvis Guide to Prospecting for Trout, Tom Rosenbauer.

In addition to his work as vice president of marketing at Orvis, Tom Rosenbauer spends most of his time on the water in pursuit of fish with a fly. He makes his home near some of the nation's most famous trout waters, the perfect laboratory for a fly-fishing writer.

The Orvis Guide to Prospecting for Trout is an invaluable resource for trout fishing during the majority of your time spent astream—fishing when there is no hatch. Rosenbauer breaks down the common trout stream, detailing the need of trout, their feeding habits, how to entice a strike, and more. The full-color photographs make the book an enjoyable read as well.

Expert

Emergers, **Carl Richards and Doug Swisher.**

Watching a trout eat a dry fly is the epitome of fly fishing for trout. Watching a trout eat *your* dry fly is a huge reason you fish. But trout are not always eating "traditional" dry flies; they are often eating emerging insects as they hatch through the water column.

Using indoor aquariums and on-stream observation, Richards and Swisher opened a new door to the fly-fishing community. *Emergers* looks at the hatches of mayflies, stoneflies, caddis, midges, damselflies, and other insects. By understanding the role emerging insects play in the feeding habits of trout, you will be a better angler.

In the Ring of the Rise, **Vincent Marinaro.**

From the author of *A Modern Dry Fly Code,* comes the quintessential book on rising trout. Marino uses high-speed photography to look at trout feeding habits from the viewpoint of the fish. The photography could stand alone as educational and entertaining. With this book, Marinaro set the bar extremely high for books on fishing dry flies.

With a large portion of the book focused on presentation, Marinaro's approach helps you understand the need of a trout to feed. But he also provides ways you can test new fly patterns and gain insight into a trout's rise form. There are also chapters on rod design and selection for targeting fish with dry flies, fishing terrestrial patterns, and tactics for fishing limestone creeks and freestone rivers.

In the Ring of the Rise is a great tool for taking your dry fly fishing to the next level.

DVDs

The DVD recommendations listed in this book are a collection of entertaining and award-winning productions. They are listed in order of their content—the list begins with mostly instructional DVDs and gravitates toward DVDs with a more entertaining focus.

***Joan Wulff's Dynamics of Fly Casting.* Presented by Miracle Productions.**

Recognized as one of the greatest instructors of fly casting, Joan Wulff, along with the great team at Miracle Productions, has created ninety minutes of easy-to-follow format and insight to improve your casting. Wulff's half-century of teaching experience comes through in this unique DVD experience. Not only will you learn what it takes to have a great cast; Wulff details tips on arm and hand movements, detailed practice routines to follow on your own, and a potpourri of tips and tricks to try.

Despite being released almost fifteen years ago, the information in this DVD is timeless. Since its release, *Wulff's Dynamics of Fly Casting* has become one of the top-selling instructional DVDs.

***Anatomy of a Trout Stream.* With Rick Hafele. Presented by Scientific Anglers.**

The title says it all. For almost an hour learn the ins and outs of what makes trout do what they do. Beginning with learning to read water and ending with proper fly selection and presentation, Hafele's years of knowledge come out in this well-filmed and knowledge-packed DVD. The DVD chronicles the needs of trout, where and why they choose prime lies, and the types of trout foods in a given stream or section of a stream.

Filmed in the 1980s, *Anatomy of a Trout Stream* feels a little dated only because of the style and quality of the picture. The information is timeless and is suited for any, and all, of today's trout fishing situations.

***Bugs of the Underworld.* With Ralph and Lisa Cutter. Presented by the California School of Fly Fishing.**

This is hands-down the best DVD presenting trout food in its natural habitat. The DVD is entertaining, with great music and amazing photography. Sir David Attenborough claims he "was enthralled," and you will be as well. The winner of several awards, including Honorable Mention at the International Wildlife Film Festival, *Bugs* chronicles the cycles of mayflies, stoneflies, caddisflies, and a few other species.

The DVD took over eleven years to produce, but the knowledge you will gain will last a lifetime.

***Advanced Nymph Fishing*. With Rick Hafele and John Smeraglio. Presented by Laughing River Productions.**

Fishing nymphs is the most misunderstood and underutilized method of fly fishing. Experienced anglers and guides guarantee that you will catch more fish day in and day out if you practice and perfect your ability to fish nymphs. To successfully fish nymphs, a thorough understanding and different approach is essential. *Advanced Nymph Fishing* helps to open the door to this different approach.

The best way to learn to fish nymphs effectively is from someone who is successful at it already—Hafele and Smeraglio are, and they are eager to share. A lot of time is given to understanding the importance of rigging your leader properly. The DVD also covers two-fly fishing, fishing sinking lines, and reading water with nymph fishing in mind. It is a two-disc set with over two hours of instruction. No longer is being uneducated an excuse for not fishing nymphs.

***Why Fly Fishing*. Miracle Productions and Jeffrey Pill. Presented by the American Museum of Fly Fishing.**

Joan Wulff, Flip Pallot, Nick Lyons, John Gierach, and more are interviewed in this unique look at the "whys" of fly fishing. By interviewing some of the well-known personalities in the sport, longtime filmmaker and talented angler Jeff Pill has brought together so many voices of the sport. And he is able to get these voices to open up and talk about why they love fishing.

We see the fun, the challenge, the art, through the eyes of some of the best and most outspoken. The only downside: Thirty minutes isn't long enough.

***Tarpon*. Featuring Jim Harrison, Thomas McGuane, Jimmy Buffett, Richard Brautigan, and Guy de la Valdene. Presented by UYA films.**

The recognizable strums of Jimmy Buffett chords accompany aerial shots of the Florida Keys as *Tarpon* opens. Like the opening credits of a mid-1980s TV drug cartel drama, this DVD defined a genre—the fly-fishing film. Instructional DVDs hold a necessary place in every fly fisher's angling library, but there are few films that depict a "fly-fishing lifestyle." *Tarpon* is one of them.

Angling and literary greats Harrison and McGuane along with the undefinable Buffett and Brautigan and a few others chronicle the seriously aimless pursuit of tarpon in the 1970s Florida Keys.

The film offers a bittersweet glimpse of what pioneering anglers went through before "everyone else was doing it." Perhaps this is what makes it so great—it is time traveling without leaving the comfort of your couch.

Fly Fishing Film Tour. Presented by The Drake magazine (www.fly fishingfilmtour.com)

Every year the editorial staff at *The Drake* gathers some of the best fly-fishing films worldwide. The collection of films then hits the road with screenings throughout the United States.

Because many new films hit the market each year, listing the best would be a cumbersome and pointless task. By viewing the *Fly Fishing Film Tour* you will learn about the newest and most entertaining films. A visit to their website provides information on where to see the film tour and information on past films and their producers.

Chapter 9

Real-Life Frugal Fly Fishers: Peter Crumbaker

Name: *Peter Crumbaker*
Location: *Seattle and the rivers and streams in the Pacific Northwest*

Growing up in the Pacific Northwest, Peter did not have to look far for water to fish. His first fishing experiences found him dabbling worms and lures in any body of water he could find.

He would often venture with his father. Amazed at his father's ability with a fly rod, Peter naturally gravitated to the long rod. After patient

A steelhead is known in the fly-fishing community as "the fish of a thousand casts."

and precise instruction from his dad, he gained confidence and improved his ability. Peter and his father would head north to the cold, clear waters of British Columbia where Peter gained more instruction from a family friend, Andy Hall. Andy was a fine fly cast, and these adventures to Canada motivated Peter to become a better angler.

Today Peter tries his tricks on the waters in and around Seattle. Not having to venture far for places to wet a line, he feels lucky to have so much water so close to home.

What level of angler would you rate yourself?
Intermediate, because I know a lot of amazing fly fishermen that cast perfectly every time. I cast well quite often, but sometimes don't. I also don't tie my own flies, and am still learning through exploration how to choose the water I'm going to fish. Still learning why I drive to this river versus that river based on weather, season, and other factors.

Where might you suggest be the best place for cheap or free but useful instruction?
On the river. Just being out there doing it yourself. When people are around, you can watch what they are doing and watch what might be working for them. You can talk with them. Because you are on the river you have the opportunity to test your new knowledge right away. But trial and error is always a good learning tool, and that happens on the river.

What one piece of gear is the most important and why?
Other than the fly I'd say your tippet. You can use cheap line and apply line cleaner to keep it afloat and in good condition. Any rod can land a fish. Any reel can bring in a fish large or small if familiar with palming the reel. But the tippet is closest to your fish. It can control the presentation of your fly. If weak you won't land any fish and sometimes ruin your day with break-off especially with big fish. If poor quality it would handle shock resistance well when setting the hook and can break. I like a high-quality tippet like Rio Fluoroflex. It is strong, thin, which is great for presentation, and has good shock resistance.

Too many anglers overlook a quality pair of polarized sunglasses, blinding themselves to a world under the reflected water.

What one piece of gear is the most overrated—in other words, what piece of gear is it okay to skimp on?

The reel. If dealing with saltwater fish, where they can run with greater power and into the infinite ocean, then the stock of the reel goes up, but in freshwater any reel will do. I landed a 12-pound fish in a river using a reel for a 3-weight and for much of my fishing career have used a 6-weight Orvis Clearwater that I bought for $15 in 2002. I have landed salmon, carp, bass, redfish, and catfish with that reel, but had it not been for the tippet I may not have landed any of them.

What are your three most overlooked pieces of gear?

Polarized sunglasses. Without these the glare off the water any time of year cannot just make it so you can't watch your line or fly, but also give you a headache trying to stare at it. And in optimal conditions can also help you to see the fish.

Water bottle. It's so important to have water when fishing for a full day, but it's not something that you want to be flopping against your leg, but also not too small so it doesn't hold much water. You either want a vest with a back pocket large enough so it's out of the way or one that basically doesn't create discomfort.

Line cleaner. I use line cleaner before fishing, and sometimes on multiday trips while fishing. It does what it's supposed to do—clean the line so it performs better. Sucks when your line continuously pulls your fly down. Typically that's because it's dirty.

How did you get to the point of knowing what you needed and what you didn't need?

By simply going fishing and talking with guys that I meet who also like fly fishing. It certainly helped working for *Northwest Fly Fishing* magazine for six years. Talking with people and learning from everyone, I realized that I honestly didn't understand a lot of my gear. Before then I was using the same rod, reel, and line for every situation from lakes to big and small rivers to beach fishing. But there is a lot out there that is not necessary, and the only way you'll know that is by fishing and thinking about what might be helpful and what isn't necessary.

Peter learned by just getting out there and doing it. Trial-and-error and self-discovery.

What are a few gear-related tips to extend the life of your gear?

I like to dry out my flies after using them so the hooks don't rust or corrode and I can get more life out of each one. Every time I take a fly off my line while fishing I put it in one box. I do this so I know which flies I have already used in case I need to rethink my approach to these fish, but also so it's easier to air out those flies when I'm done for the day.

As mentioned earlier I believe in cleaning my line. Not only does that allow it to perform the way it's supposed to, but also keeps it from cracking thus keeping it from needing to be replaced.

Moving slowly and carefully when hiking rivers or to my fishing destination. Pushing through brush is an easy way to put a hole in your waders. Walking quickly on train tracks, you can easily trip and break your rod. You can twist an ankle especially if there's a hole in your waders and your feet are a little numb. I can think of a dozen things that can happen when pushing too fast along a river or to your destination that will result in damaged gear and possibly a ruined fishing trip.

Anything else on gear?

A company that I buy a lot of my gear from is Redington. They are producing great rods, reels, waders, boots, jackets, etc., at reasonable prices. The quality is wonderful, and they have so many options I have not yet been able to find a rod that didn't fit what I was looking for. Plus, their customer service has always been good to me. Other than that I would say the most important part is going fishing, so try not to stress too much on your gear. It's easy to get over-inundated with so many options, gadgets, rod weights, lengths, etc. Try and think to yourself if the fish is still going to bite your fly if you have a double poll drag system in your reel, and also what is most comfortable to you. It can be a long day out on the water and it sucks if you aren't comfortable.

———

A huge facet of frugal fly fishing is the necessity to cut some costs. Most people aren't lucky enough to live in the Florida Keys or on the Madison

River. But that doesn't mean there isn't great fishing close to urban areas or in surprising locations.

When you first started fly fishing, was it hard to find places to fish close to home?

Nope! When I decided I wanted to start exploring new spots that my dad hadn't shown me, I simply opened up my map and started looking for rivers that didn't sound familiar. Living in Seattle, I have a lot of water nearby. I also have no problems in hitting up the city lakes that for a lot of people can often become a part of the scenery versus an opportunity. Sometimes they can also make for a wonderful view while casting to carp or bass. I was also raised on simply going after trout and sometimes salmon. So to go after different species like carp and bass really opened up the opportunities around me since those are versatile fish, and most cities will stock a lake with them to help keep it clean and the ecosystem of the lake in balance.

Do you use modern-day tools like the Internet and social networking sites to find places to fish?

Certainly. I use the Internet primarily for real-time updates on river levels, weather forecasts, and then to read any fishing reports to see what others are finding in the area. I also use it to read the newspaper of small towns I might be making a destination since they will sometimes publish fishing reports. But as for the social networking sites, I don't really get into those.

No matter if it was hard or not, how did you find places?

I started out just looking at the map and seeing what was accessible, then looking up what was interesting to me in the fishing regs to narrow down my options. But as I've grown more into the sport, I've learned a lot talking with friends at my fly-fishing club, people on the rivers or that I've met. I have also learned a lot from *Northwest Fly Fishing* magazine, and have also fished some destinations that I have read about in *Southwest Fly Fishing*. Just because it is being written about doesn't mean that people are instantly going to fish it. I have not once learned of a body of water getting too much pressure because of info published about it. What I also really like doing is hunting for the tributary waters of a river that is producing well. That's one of my tricks for finding solitude out on the river, and sometimes more manageable water if you are like myself and haven't yet adopted any spey gear.

Did you have to fish for nontraditional species? For example carp or shad or another species?

Yes, going after different species helps me to fish year-round, but have also caused me to elevate my fishing game. Going after bass, carp, rockfish, and other species causes you to further understand your gear, what works for you and doesn't, but also improves how you think of the fish. Understanding more than just fishing for trout has allowed me to actually catch larger trout!

How is that?

Learning more about bass, how they feed, where they are during different times of year, what type of water they like, what techniques have been successful for me in catching them, has all contributed to my approach to trout, and I believe I am landing larger and higher numbers of trout.

What is your best memory about discovering a new place to fish close to home or a new species close to home?

When I went out to the Olympic Peninsula car camping for four nights, I knew the water was high in most rivers and that the Coho and steelhead runs were basically done. But I hadn't yet really explored that area, and so I chose to go anyway. My plan was to use my logging roads map to try to find access to tributary water, and from there find twenty-four-hour parking because I was just sleeping in my car using the bed I had jerry-rigged in the back of my Ford Escort wagon. When I got to the Queets River, I couldn't see my feet in the water because it was so discolored. Looking at my map, I targeted a river that flowed into the Queets but looked large enough to hold a run of salmon. So I drove out to the river, found access, parked my car, made dinner, read the current issue of *Northwest Fly Fishing*, and got great sleep. When I woke up I started downriver to fish this large eddy, and after switching flies a few times got a hookup. It fought well, but I trusted my gear and happily landed 8 pounds of brightly colored Coho! I was so happy with that fish because it was new water that I had picked out using my methods, the fly I chose, and water I picked.

What is the best piece of advice for anglers wanting to fish closer to home?
Keep your eyes open while driving or commuting around town. Notice if you are crossing over a bridge what the name of that creek is underneath you. Check out those city lakes and possibly invest in a kayak or boat of some sort. With my kayak I can have it on top of my car, and be en route to the Puget Sound or a local lake within twenty minutes. Fishing closer to home typically means you have other reasons that you can't be out for a full day. Work, family, other interests, whatever. So make it easy on yourself, and if you know you want to try out some local water, just bring the essentials so you aren't bogged down with getting your gear ready, or make a purchase of something like my kayak. I have gotten more time on water with that boat than before because it has made it easier and faster to be on the water thus making it all more accessible.

A lot of anglers aspire to travel, and the natural progression for a lot of fly fishers is fishing close to home and then venturing to some far-off places. And by far off I mean a day's drive or a flight to get to the destination.

Was it a long time before you invested time and money in a destination trip?
From when I started fly fishing around eleven . . . yes! And even after college it was because I didn't have much money so those types of trips were funded by Dad. Not until I was in my late twenties did I really start putting together my own fly-fishing destination trips.

A great way to save money while fishing is to camp. Peter took that idea one step further and made his car a motel.

Have you done any DIY (do-it-yourself) trips in far-off destinations?
Yes. I have done them up in Alaska with my brother and father, and also by myself out to the Olympic Peninsula, and Montana is another regular visit of mine.

Are these DIY itineraries something you suggest to frugal fly fishers if they have never been to a destination before?
Only if they are confident in their safety, presence of mind, and take the necessary precautions; for example, know what you have to bring for food or have a plan in case of an emergency. I have an extensive first-aid kit and am considering the purchase of a firearm for such remote trips. Always be sure to tell people your itinerary. When I'm putting a car-camping or camping type of DIY trip together, I also like to pick destinations near a city so if trouble does happen I can get help.

If anglers don't feel comfortable exploring on their own, are they better spending their money on guides/lodges before they even try a DIY?
I would recommend if someone is tight on money to try out their skills on some local water and see how comfortable they feel about hooking into fish using their own methods and skills. If hooking fish isn't as much of a concern and the experience and exploration is a bigger part of it, then I would say just get out there and explore. But if you really would like to learn how to fish a new destination, guides are wonderful. You can pick their brains and learn a lot more about the area, techniques, and also that water.

For the traveling frugal fly fisher, what is some good advice?
To me the number one thing for enjoying myself is that I put the exploration and adventure before the thrill of catching a fish. That Coho I caught on the Olympic Peninsula was the only fish I hooked in the five days of fishing, but the trip itself was wonderful. To appreciate the trees, the area, conversations with new folks, standing in the water, hiking a river all day . . . it just goes on and on for me. But catching fish certainly makes a good time a better time! So definitely do your research in advance, and if you do call a fly shop for advice, to stop in and buy some flies, tippet, whatever. They may even have a river map. But to call them and ask for advice and not give anything back other than thank you is like not leaving a tip at a sit-down restaurant. Frugal is one thing but being a cheap-ass is another.

At what point in your fly-fishing development did you choose to invest in a guide?
When I had tried for years and years to land a steelhead, and for years and years came home and only got the appreciation of hiking a river. I knew it was time to hire a guide.

Was it out of necessity or because you truly wanted to learn? Was it worth it?
Definitely worth it and I learned a ton.

A few words of advice when hiring a guide?

They are there for you, so if you want to catch fish, let them know. Whatever your expectation is for the trip, let them know. Also, tipping is a part of the service but always tip whatever you are comfortable with.

———

Committing to fishing frugal is a long-term commitment. Just like getting rich doesn't typically happen overnight, understanding what it takes to be a frugal angler takes awhile and requires a different approach to fly fishing.

We've already talked about gear. Are there other things frugal fly fishers can do to save some cash but still get great fly fishing?

I rig up the car for a comfortable sleep. That's how I save a ton of money when out on the road, and also making my own dinners. I pick up chili, ravioli already in sauce, and whatever else I can make quickly since it's the

Save money by doing your own cooking. After a day of fishing it's hard to beat a hunk of meat and cold beer.

Peter Crumbaker

end of the day and I'm tired. I use a WhisperLite stove setup, and food is ready in less than twenty minutes. After that I hit up the bar!

But don't a few drinks zap up your budget?

It's worth it. There's a lot one can learn hanging out in a town with good fishing nearby at the local tavern. I personally love fishing the day with a nice buzz. Besides, you're on vacation and this is supposed to be fun! Also, don't skimp on things that are going to keep you comfortable. It's not fun if you have thin socks, or you didn't buy an insert to support your feet in your wading boots, or your raincoat is really just a wind stopper, or your waders still have holes that you can't find to patch. Be comfortable, and you'll be happy . . . and also finish the day with a nice buzz!

What would be your favorite books or websites for tips and techniques?

I use *Northwest Fly Fishing* for learning a lot of my destinations, but in the articles they also have tips and techniques from the authors. But I really don't go hunting for tips and techniques. I typically hear stuff while on the river or from the people I meet. My main tip for bettering technique is to go fishing.

If you could offer one bit of advice to someone wanting to fish more frugally, what would that be?

Don't let money hold you back from having a good time. Save up, or just really look for things on the cheap. I bought my kayak for $200, and it has brought more than that much pleasure to my fishing experiences. Be patient, go fishing, and keep your eyes open.

Chapter 10

Finding a Place to Fish: Opportunities Are Closer Than You Think

Fly fishing is a visual sport, particularly when the mind wanders to places far off and beautiful. Montana, the Florida Keys, and New Zealand tickle the inner soul. Imagine hiking from ridgetop to ridgetop in search of that perfect run, where native cutthroat trout sip emerging gray drakes. Or imagine the morning sun peeking out from the eastern horizon as the eerie dawn stillness leaves a bonefish flat. These scenes are not common

Even though few anglers venture to trout waters in winter, the colder months are great times to cast a line. The solitude is unbeatable.

Dave McCoy, Emerald Water Anglers, LLC

Some places, particularly the Pacific Northwest, require a quality rain jacket.

for every angler—they are the ultimate pursuit. They are the elusive finish line for most anglers and the daily grind for a very lucky and very small few.

A few of us were fortunate enough to be raised near these epitomical angling destinations. And for those even luckier to live in, or near, these areas, the bulk of the angling public thumbs a collective nose in your direction. However, if it were not for places like Montana or Belize or Patagonia, would fly fishing hold the appeal it does? The desire to fish an exotic location is an attainable pursuit akin to perfecting your reach cast or refining your double haul—always in the back of your mind wanting to come more forward.

In addition to a fatter wallet you must delight in things on a smaller scale. It is essential you take pride in searching out fishing opportunities close to home while trying to enjoy destination travel as a romantic notion and not a regular habit. The glass is either half-empty or half-full: schools of 10-pound carp swimming in the municipal park pond; Carp? What self-respecting angler would fly fish for carp? Get the point?

Since water covers mostly 70 percent of the earth, finding a place to wet a line is not hard. The difficulty comes in finding a place that is accessible, has water that harbors aquatic life, holds a species of fish that is willing to eat an artificial lure, aka fly, and is within a reasonable distance from your home.

Before you begin researching local waters, start with an honest critique of your angling philosophy. If you've made it this far in this book, you are committed to a little self-sacrifice for your sport—being frugal is not an easy task. It requires constant discipline and outside-the-box thinking. Along with a little twist on the norm comes a sense of adventure and a taste of the unknown. The rewards of self-discovery are plentiful as you seek out angling opportunities close to home.

Frugal fly fishers cannot afford to be purists. It makes no sense in the pocketbook. If you pass judgment on carp or bass or whitefish or any nontraditional fly rod species, then you are not being a frugal fly fisher. A fish eating your fly and a tug on the end of your line are what matter most.

Now that you've come to grips with your inner frugal fly fisher, here's a look at a few overlooked but readily accessible fly rod-able species.

Staying warm in winter is all about layers. This angler is ready for anything that a Montana winter might throw at him.

Michael Gracie; www.michaelgracie.com

Carp. The new frontier of fly fishing . . . ?

The carp is perhaps the most underrated fly rod-able species swimming in North American waters. A native of Europe and Asia, the carp has five species that anglers might catch. Despite relative differences between the five, for the purpose of getting something on the end of your line, you only need to understand that all five of the species can be lumped into one, *common grass carp*. In some areas of the United States carp are considered an invasive species and government agencies want their removal, which is another good reason to target these swimming behemoths. As Izaak Walton said of the carp in *The Compleat Angler*, "The Carp is the queen of rivers; a stately, a good, and a very subtle fish."

Although fly fishing for carp is slowly gaining popularity in the United States, the pursuit of the golden beast has many followers in Europe and many conventional angling fans in North America. In recent years a few angling groups devoted to carp and carp fishing opportunities have popped up in the United States. A few hours on the Internet will uncover information on clubs, waters, and techniques for carp. A few prominent fly anglers and experts are outspoken about the excitement carp offer. And they are right—it is hard to beat casting to a tailing 10-pound fish that, when hooked, can run you into your backing in less than thirty seconds!

Several species share the name bass, and frugal fly fishers should care about three of them: large- and small-mouth bass and striped bass. These three inhabit a massive amount of water in North America: Over 70 percent of the U.S. population lives within an hour of a piece of water holding one of these species. Large and smallmouth bass are freshwater gamefish inhabiting streams, lakes, and ponds. Striped bass, or "stripers" as they are often called, are a saltwater gamefish that during a specific time in their development are active along shorelines, beaches, and piers and freshwater lakes and rivers.

Keep an angling diary. Keep it simple. Record date, stream and section fished, weather patterns, and the most successful fly. What else you want to include is up to you. It proves a great resource down the road but also fun reading in the off-season. A little of your own record-keeping might save you some cash because you already know what is working and you might have what you need.

By its popularity and Hollywood-esque status amongst gamefish, the largemouth bass might be the most pursued freshwater gamefish swimming today. It is the state fish of Alabama, Florida, Georgia, Mississippi, and Tennessee. But even though the southern states have laid claim to the largemouth as state fish, largemouth bass still swim in water north of the Mason-Dixon Line and west of the Mississippi and can be found in all fifty states.

They are natural predators and foragers. Their aggression level is exponentially higher than most brown trout, making largemouth bass ideal targets. The only downside to largemouth bass is they spend a good portion of their life in water a little deeper than ideal for fly rodders. But if you do some homework and are willing for some adventure, you can

The Grande Ronde along the Oregon-Idaho border offers a spectacular multiday trip.

Dave McCoy, Emerald Water Anglers, LLC

target largemouth when they are in shallow waters or actively feeding on the surface. The reward is well worth the effort—a large, aggressive fish slamming a surface fly or popper and then leaping in the air trying to throw the fly.

Smallmouth bass do not inhabit as many waters as largemouth bass, but they often can be found in smaller creeks and rivers that anglers can often walk and wade-fish. Native to the waters of the upper and middle Mississippi River basin and the St. Lawrence River–Great Lakes system, smallmouth bass are ideal targets for frugal anglers. They have feeding habits similar to that of largemouth, but these smaller, yet just as aggressive, fish are more accessible than largemouth.

Smallmouth prefer clearer and cleaner habitat than largemouth and are a good indicator of a relatively healthy marine environment. Unlike largemouth bass, smallmouth have not gained a reputation for their fighting ability. That doesn't mean they should be ignored. In fact, they should be sought out.

From the Outer Banks to the Everglades to Corpus Christi to Monterrey Bay, traveling anglers spend a good chunk of money to pursue bonefish, tarpon, permit, redfish, roosterfish, and snook. Frugal fly fishers also find delight in another species swimming in these waters: the jack crevalle, commonly known as "jacks."

Jacks can be pursued by fishing from canal walls, bridges, or piers. Fly fishing for jacks is exciting: The retrieve is done by stripping the fly very fast, often done by placing the rod under the arm and stripping hand-over-hand as fast as possible. Jacks are not known for being selective, so armed with a few Clouser minnows and a spot on a seawall or pier and a good double haul, you should be in for some fun.

An entire book could be written on overlooked and ignored fly-rod-able fish. From the Rocky Mountain whitefish to shad and skipjacks, certain species have taken a backseat to trout and saltwater species. The visual nature of fly fishing should be appealing enough that seeing a tailing carp and casting to it or watching a smallmouth smash a surface-popper is enough to entice even the most traditional angler to cast a fly.

As more anglers discover fly fishing across the world, the spectrum of species targeted and methods used is growing. From cruising south Florida canals in a Honda Civic in pursuit of peacock bass to enticing a largemouth bass to eat a dry fly in New York's Central Park, there are plenty of species in plenty of places willing to eat flies cast by frugal anglers.

As unlikely as it sounds, it is true: Fly-fishing opportunities exist right before your eyes. Montana, Alaska, the Bahamas, and other locales are not the only places to wet a line *and* have a realistic chance of a tug at the other end. Most municipal ponds and creeks are home to a variety of swimming creatures. Searching out just which waters hold fish is the tricky part, but not as difficult as you might think.

Use the Internet to search your state's and town's municipal websites. Many state and town governments have done a fantastic job of detailing angling opportunities. Some states even offer maps of popular, and not so popular, angling areas. If they don't offer maps, they most likely offer a list of waters in a given area and the species that can be caught. Once you have learned about the body of water and the species, it is up to you to search out where to fish. As much as you may like all the answers given to you, some self-discovery and effort are still required.

Search out local angling clubs as well. A little extra cash spent to join a local chapter of Federation of Fly Fishers or the Coastal Conservation Association will open the door to many opportunities. You will certainly meet some fellow anglers who desire fishing close to home.

Be sure to read, on a regular basis, the outdoors section of your local newspaper. And not just the current issue. Most editions are now archived on the newspaper's website so it is possible to read up to a year's worth of angling reports or columns. Most outdoor sections have a blog written by either the outdoor editor or a staff writer at the newspaper.

A story is unlikely to have the headline "Opportunities Close to Chicago." But a column might be about taking a kid fishing or perhaps an outdoor writer's most recent adventure. In the write-up he or she might mention a certain body of water. Voila! Your next fishing trip is already planned.

Maps, atlases, and gazetteers also offer information on locations. The large-format statewide atlas and gazetteers offer large maps and listings

John Shirley; www.eaglenestlodge.com

Not at the top of anyone's list of species, the sheepshead is abundant in a lot of the saltwater fisheries in the Southeast.

of fishing spots. Published for nearly every state, these books are a cost-effective way to get information and directions for an abundance of waters.

Fly shops and sporting goods stores offer free information and advice. Most shops have a "hatch board" or information on their website on their local waters. By spending a little time, but more importantly investing a little cash in a few purchases at your nearest store, you will surely get some solid local information. It never hurts to be a regular and spend some time in the shop "shooting the breeze" with the shop staff. Most shops are happy to share information on local waters—the more you fish, the more you are likely to return and spend some money. They scratch your back, you scratch theirs.

While the Internet, local clubs, local newspapers and blogs, and local fly shops are all great resources, the best resource of them all is your own desire to search out spots. You might burn some gas and put a few miles on your rig, but you might also make some friends and find some new water to fish. Try golf course ponds, canals, city and state parks, large office complexes with ponds, and any area that has any sort of water.

Always be sure to ask permission before crossing any ground to fish any water that you might have even the remotest idea is private. If there is any doubt, ask. Nothing ruins a fishing outing more than being busted for trespassing.

If the water you want to fish is part of a large office complex or private compound of buildings, it might be a good idea to call and try to speak to someone who has the authority to grant permission. Once permission is granted, your experience is probably not going to be one of solitude. It is not every day most folks in an office environment look out their window and see someone fly fishing in the "duck pond."

When fishing these new-to-you and out-of-the-box waters, tap into your sense of adventure and your patience. It may take a few locations before you find a pond that holds fish. Or it may take a few different flies or tactics before you crack the code. But once you do, you will discover some great fishing opportunities close to home . . . and that is the core of frugal fly fishing: discovering *your* way to enjoy fly fishing.

Regional Opportunities for Frugal Fly Fishing

Northeast

States include Maine, Vermont, New Hampshire, Massachusetts, Rhode Island, Connecticut, New York, New Jersey, and Pennsylvania.

Top Five Spots
1. Small rivers and creeks in western Pennsylvania
2. Delaware River, New York and New Jersey
3. Coast of Cape Cod
4. Connecticut River, Connecticut
5. Lakes and ponds of northern Maine

Fly fishing in the Northeast is as varied as it gets. With small trout streams in Vermont and New Hampshire and coastal estuaries in New Jersey, there is never a lack for something, somewhere, to fly fish. Finding a place where an angler can stand a reasonable chance of a tug on the end of his line could literally be as close as a five-minute drive. Just because there is an abundance of water in the Northeast doesn't always mean quality fly fishing is right out your door. It usually is, but finding access sometimes requires some out-of-the-box thinking.

Unlike the western United States, finding large chunks of public land in the Northeast can be a challenge. But with this negative comes many positives—the distance between fishable water and your home is much less than the rest of the country, and because fly fishing has deep roots in the Northeast, finding accurate local information is much easier than in the Southeast or Great Plains.

As with so many things in fly fishing, your best resource is your local fly shop. If that is not an option, research on the Internet or with your state or local governments the nearest public lands or waters, and then head out.

If you need a little arm-twisting or a kick-start, here are a few places for information about fly fishing in the Northeast. The listings here are a very small sampling of the available information.

On The Water—Online (www.onthewater.com) and print edition detailing waters throughout the Northeast. A fair amount of conventional fishing is covered. But don't let that discourage you: The pictures or the articles may depict spinning rods and plugs, but fish are still fish and they will chase a fly.

Flyfishingnewengland.com—Easy-to-navigate website with little fluff—pure fishing information. Perfect for anglers wanting reports and advice and not sparkle or extraneous pizzazz.

North Eastern Fly Fishing—www.njflyfishing.com. A web forum with an abundance of topics, most of which are where and when to go fishing.

Mid-Atlantic
States include Delaware, Maryland, Virginia, North Carolina, and West Virginia.

Top Five Spots
1. Shenandoah River, Virginia
2. Shorelines of Maryland and Virginia

3. Trout streams in West Virginia
4. Western North Carolina
5. Outer Banks, North Carolina

States in the Mid-Atlantic region offer a unique mix of cold-water fishing with some exciting year-round saltwater fly fishing. All the states are home to trout fishing, which provides ample opportunity for the frugal fly fisher. But for anglers willing to pursue some out-of-the-box fly fishing, a whole new window of fishing opens up in the Mid-Atlantic. From small- and largemouth bass to striped bass in rivers and along the shoreline, anglers from Baltimore to Charlotte could truly find fish to cast to every day of the year.

Because the spine of the Appalachian Mountains cuts through the heart of this region, public lands are more easily found than in the Northeast. The forest lands in the Appalachian Mountains offer access to

Smallmouth can be found in a variety of Mid-Atlantic waters.

Judson Conway: www.ecoflyfishing.com

hundred of miles of trout streams. The abundant and accessible Atlantic coastline is a bona fide option.

Like the Northeast, finding access requires a little homework. Here are a few resources to get you started.

Mid-Atlantic Game and Fish—www.midatlanticgameandfish.com. This site is part of the larger Game and Fish Network of online and print media. But they offer seasonal and regional information.

Mid-Atlantic Council of the Federation of Fly Fishers—www.macfff .org. One of the regional councils of the Federation of Fly Fishers, they are a great resource. From salt to smallmouth, by joining this group you will open the door to lots of opportunities in the region.

Virginia Coastal Fly Fishers—www.vcfa.org. Fishing mostly Virginia and North Carolina waters, this club is dedicated to education and opportunity. If you live in Virginia or North Carolina, or fish in either state (Marylanders?), this is a great resource and even better club to join.

Southeast

States include Kentucky, Tennessee, Arkansas, Mississippi, Louisiana, Mississippi, Alabama, Georgia, South Carolina, and Florida.

Top Five Spots
1. Florida Keys
2. Georgia bass lakes
3. East Tennessee trout creeks and rivers
4. Ozark Mountains, Arkansas
5. Louisiana Gulf Coast

Fly fishing in the Southeast is an adventure. From the southern end of the Appalachian Mountains to the flats of the Florida Keys to the world-record-producing tailwaters of Arkansas, the Southeast could be considered an angler's paradise. Compared to the American West, these angling opportunities are relatively close—it is not unrealistic to catch 5-pound brown trout one day and in a day's drive cast to tailing redfish.

If we are trying to be frugal fly fishers, staying close to home is key to keeping your cash, and the Southeast is perfect for staying close to home because water, and access, abounds. With thousands of miles of coastline and more public lands than the Midwest and Great Plains combined, it's no wonder the Southeast has a reputation for being an outdoor playground. Professional bass anglers spend most of the circuit in the Southeast, and there's good reason for frugal fly fishers to do the same.

There is one big drawback for fly fishers in most of the Southeast, with Florida being the only exception. The number of people *actually* fly fishing is quite small when compared to the numbers of anglers who fish conventionally. The reason is obvious—fly fishing was late to come to this part of the country. Florida, particularly the Florida Keys, holds a deep-rooted fly fishing tradition, but it is a relatively light spot on an otherwise dark angling map. As more anglers across the Southeast look to stay closer to home, more opportunities are opening up.

Here are a few organizations to point you in the right direction. But keep in mind there are hundreds of local angling clubs and regional fly shops in the Southeast.

Jack crevalle serves up some overlooked fly fishing in the southeastern salt.

Southeast Fly Fishing Forum—www.southeastflyfishing.com. From boats to bluegills to bonefish, this forum of anglers is dedicated to fishing the Southeast. The name says it all.

Florida Fly Fishing Association—www.floridaflyfishing.org. Strictly Florida anglers, but a good resource for residents or visiting anglers.

Southeastern Council of the Federation of Fly Fishers—www.fffsec .org. Organization of anglers committed to fly fishing in the Southeast. Education, conservation, and camaraderie.

Southern Council of the Federation of Fly Fishers—www.southern councilfff.org. Membership includes a few states outside of the Southeast region, but the information and networking for the region is useful.

Florida Council of the Federation of Fly Fishers—www.fff-florida.org. Florida-only branch of the Federation of Fly Fishers.

Midwest

States include Minnesota, Iowa, Wisconsin, Missouri, Illinois, Indiana, Michigan, and Ohio.

Top Five Spots
1. Northern Michigan trout streams and steelhead
2. Driftless area of Iowa, Minnesota, and Wisconsin
3. Minnesota lakes and ponds
4. Ozarks, Missouri
5. Ohio, Great Lakes steelhead

This region is home to famous places like Michigan's Au Sable and Minnesota's lakes. This region is also home to thousands of bass and warmwater ponds that hold fish who may have never seen a fly. Add to these already productive waters the countless miles of trout streams in the Driftless area, and southern Missouri and Midwest frugal anglers need not travel far to find a place to cast a fly.

This region is also home to runs of Great Lakes steelhead. With hundreds of small creeks and rivers flowing into Lakes Superior, Michigan, and Erie, nearby anglers might time it right and enjoy some remarkable fishing for large trout.

Andy Sabota: www.Midwestflyworks.com

Fly fishing for trout in the Midwest is a well-kept secret—and the hard-core anglers there do their part to make sure the quality remains.

Sight-fishing for carp is growing in interest as well in many areas of the Great Lakes. In addition to carp, numerous ponds and sections of rivers offer small- and largemouth bass.

Public lands are not as abundant in the Midwest as in the Southeast or Rocky Mountains, but inquire locally or on the Internet and you will be surprised how much water is available. As always, be sure to obey all private property laws, and when in doubt, always ask permission.

If access is hard to find, try any one of these organizations for more information.

Midwest Fly Fishing—www.mwfly.com. Online and print media with an abundance of information.

Midwest Fly Fish—www.midwestflyfish.com. Check out their blog for information on hatches, gear, and all things related to fly fishing in the Midwest.

Southern Council of the Federation of Fly Fishers—www.southern councilfff.org. This site includes information and social networking for fly fishing in Missouri.

114

Great Lakes Council of the Federation of Fly Fishers—www.fffglc.org. One of the oldest regional councils of the FFF. There is a lot of water in this region. By joining the Great Lakes Council you will have one foot in the door to exploring more effectively.

Great Plains

States include North and South Dakota, Nebraska, Kansas, Oklahoma, and Texas.

Top Five Spots

1. Texas Gulf Coast around Corpus Christi and South Padre Island
2. Black Hills of South Dakota
3. Kansas bass lakes and ponds
4. Oklahoma trout (yes, there are trout in Oklahoma)
5. Texas Hill Country

This region cuts down the middle of the United States. It is long in geography and long in options, some traditional, some not as traditional, for

John Shirley; www.eaglenestlodge.com

Redfish abound in the Texas Gulf Coast. Happy angler. Not-so-happy redfish.

anglers. There are trout in places you wouldn't normally think to find trout. Some of the best sight-fishing for tailing redfish in the world occurs along the Texas Gulf Coast, and carp fishing is good along the Missouri River, which runs the entire length of this region.

Stretching from the U.S.-Canada border in North Dakota down to the Mexican border in southern Texas, this region has surprisingly little public land, although there are numerous state parks scattered throughout the region. State, city, and county lands are going to be your best bets for ease of access. Despite little access, finding great fishing is not as difficult as it may seem. It will take some legwork and some patience, but most water in the region holds fish.

Contact or join any of the following organizations for more information.

Texas Fly Fishing—www.texasflyfishing.com. An informative site for fly fishing in Texas.

Southern Council of the Federation of Fly Fishers—www.southern councilfff.org. Your best resource for fly fishing in Texas, Nebraska, Oklahoma, and Kansas.

Texas Fly Fishers—www.texasflyfishers.org. A Houston-based organization, but members fish and report from everywhere in the region.

Southwest

States include Colorado, Utah, Nevada, New Mexico, Arizona, and Southern California.

Top Five Spots

1. Roaring Fork Valley, Colorado
2. Taos area, New Mexico
3. Green River, Utah
4. Northern Front Range, Colorado
5. Southern California bass fishing

Most frugal anglers in the Southwest are going to target trout. Most likely you live in one of the larger cities in this region. These cities are often a long drive from quality trout waters, but that doesn't mean you have to drive two hours to fish—in fact, with some nontraditional thinking you

Small streams like this abound in the Southwest. Thanks to an abundance of public lands, access is easy. Despite ease of access, anglers may find solitude.

might find great fishing in your neighborhood. Of course it is hard to beat fishing in the beauty of Colorado's majestic mountains, but a tug on your line feels great whether it's a trout or a panfish.

Access in this region is often easy to find as public lands are plentiful. Most rivers flow through federal or state lands, and there are good networks of roads. If you are considering fishing ponds or lakes, access might be a little more difficult, but with a little legwork you should be fishing sooner rather than later.

In Southern California some saltwater fly-fishing opportunities exist, but they are relatively unexplored—which can be a boom or a bust for an individual frugal fly fisher with an adventuresome spirit.

For more information on this region, look into these organizations.

Colorado Fishing Network—www.coloradofishing.net. Name pretty much says it all. Great map feature to really give you a head start.

Southwestern Council of the Federation of Fly Fishers—www.south westcouncilfff.org. Southern California and Nevada members and clubs of the Federation of Fly Fishers. Great networking organization for finding places to fish.

New Mexico Fly Fishing—www.new-mexico-fishing.com. Information on the rivers and lakes of northern New Mexico.

Northern Rocky Mountains

States include Montana, Wyoming, and Idaho.

Top Five Spots

1. Yellowstone National Park
2. Bighorn River, Montana
3. Henry's Fork, Idaho
4. Missouri River, Montana
5. Madison River, Montana

Montana, Wyoming, and Idaho conjure up images of the quintessential fly-fishing experience—sparkling rivers, snowcapped peaks, and large jumping trout. And yes, they have an abundance of all three. They also offer a wide array of easily accessible fly-fishing waters. So it's no mystery why most, if not all, anglers across the United States want to venture to this region someday, if they have not already.

For frugal fly fishers, this region is home to a wide array of waters, from high mountain small streams to large rivers at lower elevations. As more anglers fish the waters in these states, more nontraditional fly-fishing opportunities are popping up as well. From sight-fishing grasshopper dry flies to carp to stripping popping bugs for northern pike, trout anglers are finding other fish to target. The region is also home to a few steelhead runs in a few Idaho rivers.

This region is home to some famous waters—Henry's Fork, the South Fork of the Snake, the Madison, the Yellowstone, and others. This region is such a popular destination, finding information on its fishing is easy. Here are just a few of the resources available.

Big Sky Fishing—www.bigskyfishing.com. The best resource for information about fishing in Montana, period.

Wyoming on the Fly—www.wyomingonthefly.com. Serves up ridiculous amounts of information.

Andy Sabota: www.Midwestflyworks.com

The Yellowstone River in Montana is a destination fishery for many and home for a lucky few.

Idaho Fly Fishing Report—www.idahoflyfishingreport.com. Just that—reports and information on Idaho's fly fishing.

Pacific Northwest and Alaska

States include Alaska, Washington, Oregon, and Northern California.

Top Five Spots

1. Kenai Peninsula, Alaska
2. Deschutes River, Oregon
3. Southeast Alaska steelhead rivers
4. Hat Creek, California
5. Umpqua River, Oregon

This region is most known for its steelhead and salmon fishing. Although there is an abundance of water in this region, learning to fish the waters successfully truly takes a lifetime of knowledge. For most of the waters in this region, their fishing is predicated on what, and when, fish are "running" in them. On any given day in a lot of these streams there can be a few different species of salmon, steelhead, and cutthroat trout, or nothing at all. The secret to unlocking the mystery: local knowledge and time on the water.

Alaska is home to thousands of miles of fishable rivers and creeks. Washington, Oregon, and California have plentiful opportunities as well.

A journey to Alaska may be the trip of a lifetime for many anglers. It's easy to see why: The fish of a lifetime can be caught there.

In all four states public access is easy to come by. Knowing if you are in the right place at the right time is another story altogether.

Should trout, salmon, or steelhead get you down in the angling dumps, there are plenty of ponds and lakes that hold bass, pike, and a few other species. With as much water that exists in this region, finding a place to fish is never a problem—but finding water that is *home* to fish at that moment is a whole other ballgame.

To help you in your fish-finding endeavors, here are a few resources.
Alaska's Fly Fishing Network—www.alaskaflyfish.net. Their charts and reports are updated regularly and offer reliable information.
Washington Fly Fishing—www.washingtonflyfishing.com. Hands-down the best resource for fly fishing in Washington.
The Caddis Fly: Oregon Fly Fishing Blog—www.oregonflyfishingblog .com. A great tool for learning to fish Oregon's diverse fisheries. Some great information on flies, too.

Northern California Council of Fly Fishers—www.nccfff.org.
Information on rivers, outings, and more from Northern California's
Federation of Fly Fishers' main chapter.

Hawaii

Hawaii may appear to be an imposing fishery to the frugal angler: big
water, big waves, territorial local anglers, tales of giant bonefish, and a
severely depleted inshore fishery hammered by years of over-fishing. But
what Hawaii may lack in first impressions, it makes up for once you learn
a little more.

A few of the islands have shallow water flats where bonefish, trevally,
and a few other species swim. Some of the bonefish are *big,* too. The state
record for a line and reel landed bonefish is over 18 pounds and stood
as the world record for years. On average the bonefish are bigger than in
Florida, the Bahamas, and the Caribbean.

For anglers wishing to fish in Hawaii, it is best to think of each individual island as its own fishery. Here's a quick breakdown:

Hawaii is home to some massive bonefish, like this off Oahu.

Oahu: There are ample opportunities for the wading angler here, however the tides and winds are fickle, so local knowledge is crucial. The bonefishery is world class and 10-pounders can be landed by a good angler armed with proper knowledge—and most likely a good guide.

Kauai: Bonefish flats and wading anglers can find a few places to cast to cruising fish. There are also opportunities for jacks and other species if you want to hike in-and-out of coral heads.

Molokai: Huge bonefish and trevally and miles of inner reef flats, but not great access. Fishing is difficult because of the need to understand the winds and the tides.

Big Island: No real flats opportunities here, but some great offshore fishing opportunities.

Lanai: Some flats are wade-able, but very difficult to access.

Maui: No flats, no guides, and a severely depleted inshore fishery.

And here's another great resource for Hawaii fly fishing: *Hawaii Bonefishing*—www.Hawaiibonefishing.com. These guys know Hawaii. As guides on Oahu and Kaui, Coach Duff and Rob Arita are willing to offer-up information on Hawaii's unique fishing. To truly understand Hawaii fly fishing, it is worth it to book a day with either.

Chapter 11

Real-Life Frugal Fly Fishers: Peter McDonald

Name: *Peter McDonald*
Location: *Northeast*
Blog or website: *fishingjones.com*

After college, Peter chased cheap rent and visited plenty of bars while looking for work in New York City. For a short while he landed in Hoboken—a place highly unregarded as a bastion for fly fishing. In a typical post-college search for meaning, Peter shared an apartment with two brothers who were

Peter McDonald with a monster northeast saltwater striped bass.

123

into hunting and fishing. As the saying goes, "If you can make it in Hoboken . . ." Today, Peter still makes his home in the Northeast. He can be found searching out new, close-to-home fishing options however out-of-the-box they may be. He's not against tossing a fly into a roadside ditch . . . you never know what type of fish is lurking in ditches.

You mentioned these two brothers in Hoboken. Were they responsible for getting you hooked on fly fishing?
I shared an apartment with them. The older brother had gotten into fly fishing and he turned his brother and me onto it. Right around then, I got a Cortland 6-weight starter kit as a gift. It came in this plastic packaging and was pre-rigged with a clicker reel that had no drag; you just palmed it to stop a fish if it came to that.

Where did you first use your new toy?
There was a park about forty minutes away from our apartment with stocked trout. My roommates took me there, showed me how to tie on a nymph, and we all went on our way. That first day I caught a little creek chub about 5 inches long. It took me a year of trying to catch another fish on fly.

Were you frustrated trying to learn?
I just couldn't get it to work but I really wanted to. I stuck with it until one day we were fishing this trout stream in New York and a trout decided to eat my wooly bugger.

From whom did you learn the bulk of your fly-fishing skills?
Well, I bought my first pair of neoprenes and the brothers I roomed with told me you wear the gravel guards on your elbows. Not a huge help. Mostly a lot of just going with friends who were also learning and figuring it out together.

Were there any shops or groups that you found helpful?
I used to go to these two fly shops in New York City, Orvis and the Urban

Angler, and ask a million dumb questions, then buy a couple flies so as not to be totally parasitic.

So you pretty much learned by trial and error and just being patient?
I really started figuring it out on my own, fishing for sunfish and Rockies with a small popper up on my family's summer place on the St. Lawrence River.

What, or who, was your biggest motivator when you were trying to learn?
A combination of things. *A River Runs Through It* had recently come out as a movie, but my dad gave me the book as a gift so I read that first. Watching *Walker's Cay Chronicles,* which was just such a different fishing show, and wanting to fish like Flip Pallot and his buddy Dozer. The whole vibe of fly fishing really appealed to me. But mostly just taking it up with a group of friends. For some reason, on a personal level, something about it felt right to me and I really wanted to make it work.

What level of angler would you rate yourself?
Competent.

Where might you suggest be the best place for cheap or free but useful instruction?
Going into the fly shops and asking stupid questions. You won't always get an answer, and may suffer through a little condescension, but you don't have to tell them your name.

Same goes for being on the water, seeing someone do it well and then watching them for a while, and then, a lot of times I tried to catch up with them and ask them about it.

When you would approach these strangers streamside, were they helpful?
Usually I found people to be pretty receptive immediately after they landed a fish. Usually they're pumped up about it and it was easy to ask a few questions. But most of the time I'd ask people I ran into near the parking lot at the end of the day. I didn't want to bother people actually in the act of fishing as the last thing I wanted to be responsible for was them missing a fish or spooking their stretch of water.

———

Fly-fishing gear has come a long way. Today, anglers have to sift through hundreds of rod models, a bunch of reels, and more gadgets than imaginable. Understanding gear today is a challenge much more daunting than ten or twenty years ago.

What one piece of gear is the most important and why?
That's a tough question. I used to think it was the rod, but I've had more bad experiences with crappy fly line than crappy rods, or using the wrong fly line for a situation, so I'm not sure.

Would you say a quality fly line is perhaps just as important as a quality rod?
Based on some of the experiences I've had. You know how cheap line constantly coils back on itself and just doesn't flow well from the rod? I had a day of bonefishing nearly ruined because I forgot to change out this old beat-up floating line, and as we were walking the flats, it kept sinking and catching on coral and grass. Eventually my guide just held it in his hands and walked next to me, like a caddy.

What piece of gear is the most overrated—in other words, what piece of gear is it okay to skimp on?
Before I started saltwater fly fishing, I would have said the reel, but fishing for stuff that gets into the backing changes that equation. Perhaps a vest?

What are the three most overlooked pieces of gear, in order of their importance and why?
1. Polarized sunglasses. A lot of people don't like to spend money on them because they drop them, scratch them, or lose them all the time. I used to get the $20 glasses with spray-on polarization; then I got a high-end pair and they opened up what I could see in the water tenfold.
2. Buff. Hard to imagine spending twenty bucks on a glorified head

sock, but I used to constantly get sunscreen in my eyes or on my sunglass lenses and this solves both problems.

3. Rain gear. Nothing ruins a day faster than discovering your outerwear isn't quite waterproof and/or windproof.

Do you have any personal experiences where perhaps inexpensive gear worked just as well as high-priced gear?

I'm not really a huge gear guy. Although I learned to appreciate inexpensive gear fishing with guide Scott Hamilton off Palm Beach, Florida. He had all these plastic reels that cost like $30 or something, and he'd use them until the drag burned and either fix it or buy a new one. We caught false albies and spinner sharks and dolphin and other fish that take you into your backing and never had a problem.

What's a gear-related tip to extend the life of your gear?

If I'm at a hotel, I always throw my gear in the bathtub. You know, to wash off the dirt and grime.

Quality rain gear allowed this angler to stay out longer, which allowed a fish like this to be caught.

A lot of what frugal fly fishers need to be good at is sniffing out fishing opportunities close to home. With all the sexy marketing that travel companies have out there in the fly-fishing world, a lot of anglers look down upon fishing close to home. That is not to say that traveling to the Bahamas or Christmas Island isn't a great thing. There have to be closer-to-home options out there.

When you first started fly fishing, was it hard to find places to fish close to home?
Since I lived in Hoboken, New Jersey, and then in Manhattan, but hadn't clued into the northeast saltwater fishery, yeah, it really was. Fishing usually involved at least an hour's drive.

Do you use modern-day tools like the Internet and/or social networking sites?
I've been blogging for seven years and have met a lot of people that way, but I don't use Facebook or forums or anything nearly as much as I should. When I started, the Internet was still pretty much dial-up, so it was easier to go buy a magazine.

No matter if it was hard or not, how did you find places?
I had friends who took me to a couple of trout streams outside New York City that they knew. When I lived in the city, this one guy at the Orvis store told me you could fly fish for bass in Central Park. I could walk from my apartment or take the subway two stops and be fishing, or at least casting. Every now and then I'd go and catch little largemouth, sunfish, and crappie. It opened a whole new world for me as far as thinking what could be fishable water.

You mentioned a little about "ditchin'" around where you live now and in Florida. How did you discover it, what keeps you doing it?
The whole Central Park thing started me looking into ponds or little bodies of water you'd drive by and see if there were fish.

But what about ditchin'?

I started working for *Boating Magazine* in 1998 and went down to Florida about once or twice a month, on average. I'd have all these trips down there, but the primary focus was not fishing. So I'd pack a rod tube and try to fish whenever I had a spare moment. I grew up down there and I'd visit one of my best buds. He had divorced parents, his mom lived on a golf course in Palm Beach and his dad lived on a lake and canal system near Ft. Lauderdale. I'd meet up with him after my work was over and we'd fish both spots for bass with poppers. One day at his dad's place, his popper got destroyed by an explosion I'd never seen from a largemouth. I was fishing a baitfish pattern and right after that I watched a 3-pound peacock bass blast out of these lily pads and just crush my fly. Then it started going nuts. After that, and getting a look at its bright orange accents, I fell in love with peacock bass. State biologists introduced butterfly peacocks in the 1990s to combat other invasive species. They've thrived in Miami and Ft. Lauderdale.

So, you don't necessarily need a boat to fly fish in South Florida?

In South Florida it's hard to fish saltwater many places without a boat, but the whole interior is crisscrossed with canals and little man-made lakes and ponds all the way out to the Everglades. On many of these trips I would have two or three spare hours, so I'd pack a freshwater travel rod and drive around to all these little bodies of water, figuring it out. I had heard about Steve Kantner, who called himself the "Land Captain." He specialized in finding snook and baby tarpon and grass carp for his clients by driving them around. I never fished with him but that also inspired me.

What species of fish did you catch?

I started catching all kinds of fish: peacock bass, Mayan cichlids, largemouth bass, bream. Another angler introduced me to a stretch of water filled with snakeheads, and I started fishing for them. Also oscars. I caught a bowfin on the fly. It became a challenge, pulling into office building parking lots, fast food joints, churches, supermarkets, and fishing the ditches running in front of or behind them.

The beautiful peacock bass is a delight to catch. They hit on the surface, jump when hooked, and can be in roadside ditches.

Back home in New York, what type of fishing were you doing if you were not in a boat?

I used to have access to a boat, so I spent most of my fishing time chasing striped bass, blues, albies, and so on. Losing boat access about a year and a half ago and becoming a parent has curtailed my fishing time and range. I used to get on a boat and go all day; now I have typically three-hour windows to head to the beach. It's harder to be productive that way.

Do you adapt your approach to fishing now that you have less time?

I started taking what I learned ditch fishing in Florida and applying it here. I found a panfish pond fifteen minutes from my house, two places nearby where you can catch largemouth once in a while, and three spots that hold carp, though I haven't landed a carp yet. Those fish are freaks. I'm trying to learn the carp game and hope it translates into landing fish next season.

What is your best story or memory about discovering a new place to fish close to home or a new species close to home?

I'd say in Florida, I drove to this spot where a canal runs along a local road that was under construction. No reasonable person would have the expectation of catching a fish there. I walked the bank, and the construction crew on the road stopped to watch me. I made a cast into this culvert with a big storm pipe, made one strip, and a big peacock bass blasted the fly and exploded out of the water. The construction crew started cheering and five or six guys ran down to the water to root me on.

What is the best piece of advice for anglers wanting to fish closer to home?

Find water and study it and try fishing it. See what's in there. There may not be glamour species around, but it's a good way to be out there casting, feeling a tug, and keeping your skills sharp, or learning new skills.

You mention you were caught with the saltwater bug. The natural progression for a lot of fly fishers is fishing close to home and then

Peter McDonald; www.fishingjones.com

Similar to a peacock bass, but more exotic, the Mayan cichlid is overlooked by most mainstream anglers.

venturing to far-off places. And by far off I mean a day's drive or more of a flight to get to the destination.

Was it a long time before you invested time and money in a destination trip? Was it worth the money spent?

But yeah, totally worth it. The first destination trip I took was for bonefish in Bimini. Not quintessential Bahamas lodge-based fishing, but it was still a destination deal. I had tried a few times in the Keys, for half-day trips, and struck out. Even with a guide, it takes time to figure out what the hell you're looking for. Going to a place with less angling pressure and with more time to understand what's happening on the flats was amazing. It's kind of like the saying, "You don't know what you don't know until you know it." That's why it's worth taking at least three days or a whole week if you can, because the early part of the trip gets eaten up by the learning curve.

Have you done any DIY trips in far-off destinations?

I do those Florida trips all the time, and have brought rods to and done DIY research for places where I've gone not specifically to fish but on family vacations.

I have a couple of DIY trips that I do with different groups of friends every year. But those always involve someone with local knowledge.

Are these DIY itineraries something you suggest to frugal fly fishers if they have never been to a destination before?

No. I'd hire a guide. Or at least go with someone who's familiar with the area. You can't replace local knowledge. If you try to do a DIY trip, first make sure to see if it's even possible where you're trying to go. Depending on where you're going, it may be a question of access.

For the traveling frugal fly fisher, what might be your top words of advice?

I bought all these cheap travel accessories—a knockoff imitation Boga grip, plyers, fly boxes—that I don't care if they get lost or stolen out of my checked bag. I actually do throw a bunch of flies in a Ziploc sometimes.

I also have cheap rods and reels I bring for the same reason, no big deal if they get lost or stolen.

At what point in your fly fishing development did you choose to invest in a guide?

About three or four years into it, I think the first guide I ever hired was Scott Hamilton in Palm Beach, a night trip fishing for snook then fishing for jack crevalle and such at sunrise. It was totally worth it. From that one trip I learned a few new knots, fly patterns, techniques for fighting and landing bigger fish. Good guides are the guys on the water every day, and you can learn so much from a good guide.

Do you have any words of advice for anglers looking to hire a guide for the first time?

Try to verify if the person is legit and doesn't mind working with inexperienced anglers, or anglers not familiar with that type of fishing.

Frugal anglers like Peter have made it an art to pare down their fly selections. Here is a large box of saltwater flies and next to it a smaller box—store your flies in larger boxes and then when you venture out for a day of fishing, use a smaller box. You spend less money on fly boxes.

Tying great knots doesn't happen overnight. It takes practice, practice, practice.

For a lot of frugal fly fishers, the sport is relatively new. Once they've made the leap and purchased some basic gear, they still have to spend money to actually "go" fishing—that's even true for experienced anglers. The simple act of going fishing costs money. Over time you have probably developed a few tricks to help stretch your fishing dollar.

What would be your favorite books or websites for tips and techniques?
Midcurrent.com, Lefty Kreh's *Fly Fishing in Saltwater,* Rich Murphy's *Fly Fishing for Striped Bass.*

We've already talked about gear. What are other things frugal fly fishers can do to save some cash but still get great fly fishing?

I usually rent economy cars. A lot of times they're out of them at the airport and you get a free upgrade. Crash at friends' houses. I usually buy breakfast and lunch at 7-Eleven or gas stations and save big on the food budget. I've bartered trips with guys, sometimes on purpose, sometimes by default. I had this one guided trip booked in Florida where my buddy cancelled, so I posted splitting a trip on one of the forums. This guy responded and said he'd take me snook fishing on his boat the day before, if I took him offshore fishing on my guided trip. So I wound up getting two trips for the price of one. Sometimes it is something as simple as offering gas money or to buy beers back at the dock.

Chapter 12

Taking It to the Next Level: Travel, Boats, and Guides

Rods, reels, fly lines, instructional books, where-to guide books . . . If you've dropped a lot of money on gear and knowledge, you may not have much left to spend on travel, boats, or guides. But since fly fishing is a lifelong pursuit, most of us are going to need some information about how best to drop the occasional wad of cash on a few luxuries of fly fishing.

Added to the obvious rewards of fishing frugal—new-found fishing holes close to home, great deals on fancy reels, new friendships at a local angling club—a long-term reward for the frugal angler might be the opportunity to splurge on a trip to an exotic locale, the purchase of a boat, or a few days with an expert guide. At some point in the pursuit of your passion, you owe it to yourself to spoil yourself. Unlike a spending spree to Vegas, money spent on travel, a boat, or a guide is not all for naught—it will make you a better angler and create some lasting memories.

A simple Internet search or thumb through a fly-fishing magazine serves up an abundance of destinations: Alaska, Belize, Montana, Argentina, Russia, the Indian Ocean. All of these are spectacular areas of the world to wet a line. And the marketing materials will lead you to believe that their destination is the greatest on earth. How can that be? Is Chilean Patagonia better than New Zealand's South Island? Are the bonefish faster in Ascension Bay than in the Bahamas?

Rent It: Most shops and lodges offer rod rentals. If you only need a 9-weight for one week, rent it rather than buy. The money you save will buy you an extra day with a guide.

The frugal fly fisher could possibly lose his mind trying to choose

136

Guides earn their money by passing on local knowledge. From rigging up to rowing you down the river, a good guide has a loyal following and is worth every penny.

one destination to fish, *if* he is fortunate to fish any of these far-off destinations. Fishing an exotic location is a real possibility if you've made reasonable decisions on gear and you already fish close to home. You should take into account some basic ideals when choosing a destination: a realistic evaluation of your skill level, the cost of travel to get to a given location, logistics and amenities once there, and the need to update or add to your gear arsenal.

Do not waste a few hundred to a thousand dollars in travel across the globe if your 30-foot cast won't cut it on the gin-clear streams of New Zealand. An honest look at your own skill level is the first step in deciding where to travel and what to fish for. Even if you've always wanted to fly fish for bonefish, if you cannot cast 40 feet and farther on a consistent basis, then you should practice before you invest money in a trip.

If you are not a strong wader, then perhaps a steelhead trip or a trip to a high-mountain area is not a good idea. Before you make any trip,

A guide on the saltwater flats allows you more access and a set of time-tested eyes for spotting tails or laid-up fish.

Mike Guerin; www.fullcircleoutfitters.com

research the necessary skills and be *honest* in your assessment of *your* skills. If you don't, you may spend a lot of money for boat rides and long walks in the mountains.

Some destinations simply cost more to get to than others. Argentina is always going to cost more to get to than Belize because Argentina is farther away. You might be able to find the occasional screaming deal on a flight to the Southern Hemisphere, but in most cases destinations in the Northern and Western Hemispheres are where you will plan to visit. When researching saltwater destinations, Mexico and the Bahamas have an abundance of flights to an assortment of fishing areas, plus both countries can be reached via nonstop flights from most U.S. hub cities. Alaska is reasonably priced despite its distance from the lower 48 states, but from areas other than the West Coast, travel time is quite long. Central American and Caribbean destinations like Costa Rica, Belize, and Venezuela are becoming easier to get to but, when comparing costs, are slightly more expensive than Mexico and the Bahamas.

As new destinations pop up—like the Seychelles, Russia's Kamchatka peninsula, Christmas Island, and southern Africa—as fantastic as they would be to visit, for the frugal fly fisher it is important to keep things in perspective. A trip to the Okavango Delta in Botswana for tiger fish makes great fodder for the imagination, but the reality is most frugal fly fishers will never visit the swampy grasslands and cast among hippos and crocodiles. For those fortunate enough to do so, we only hope they write and share their experiences.

Fly fishing, of course, is only one aspect of a destination trip. You are going to need a place to sleep, food to eat, and transportation to and from fishing spots. Logistics and support services are other factors to consider when planning a trip. Many far-off destinations are only available through full-service, all-inclusive lodges. Some destinations are a little more user-friendly for anglers willing to book and arrange their own lodging or cook their own meals. As more anglers travel to more places throughout the world, lodge-only locations are now becoming more frugal friendly.

In the past it took a lot of research to find places in the Bahamas where an angler could walk-wade, find lodging, and eat on his own. This is not to diminish the lodge experience—in fact, it could steer people toward the lodge experience. Whether you choose a lodge-based destination trip or a trip where you arrange your own lodging and meals depends on a few things.

Time versus money is a question to ask yourself. And the time involved is typically in the planning stage of

Ship-It Before You Go: If you are flying to a destination and it's possible to ship your gear before you fly, do it. Given high baggage fees and unreliable airline baggage services, shipping your gear saves you hassle and worry.

the trip. For so many anglers, life is busy. With jobs, work, and families, finding fishing time is a challenge in itself. Now factor in time researching a destination a few thousand miles away. It is not an easy task. The Internet is a great tool to find places where lots of people have already been, but you may wish to travel to places devoid of crowds. Fortunately, not all destinations have information readily available on the Internet—there are still a few places left in the angling world that are not on Facebook or Twitter, yet.

If you enjoy spending countless hours researching lodging and meal-planning, then more power to you. If spending time working or being with friends and family is more important than the money you can budget for a trip, then you might want to consider a lodge or an all-inclusive trip.

Whether you self-identify as a frugal fly fisherman or not, the ability to easily plan a trip should enter into your decision-making process regarding where to go. Some areas have a little more angling infrastructure in place, making it easier to plan a trip. For example there are islands in the Bahamas with independent guides, accessible walk-wade flats, lots

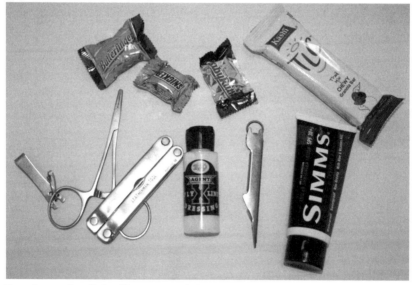

Venturing to a far-off place? Be sure to pack these essential items: forceps and nippers; fly dressing; multitool; nail-knot tool; sunscreen; and an assortment of snacks. These items are also must-haves for your fishing close to home.

of lodging options, and a wide array of dining options. But if you want to fish for tarpon in Mexico, you might be looking at a different scenario altogether.

If you do not have the time to research and arrange, there are many first-class destination fly-fishing travel services in business today. They offer complete booking services and trip planning suggestions. All offer their booking services completely free of charge. When thinking about a destination trip, working with one of these services is always a good idea.

Call Ahead: Just before your trip, call ahead and speak with your guide, the lodge, or a local shop. Their first-hand knowledge may help with any last-minute planning. You can always check things on the Internet, but first-hand local knowledge can't be beat.

Most far-off destinations will require some gear updates or additions, especially saltwater destinations. You may need to buy a new rod, a few new fly lines, and certainly some new flies. If you are a member of an angling club or have a good relationship with your local fly shop, you can probably find anglers who own what you may need. They could be a resource to borrow or rent the necessary gear. Since a new rod costs a few hundred dollars and up, asking around might save you some serious cash—cash that could buy you an extra day on a saltwater flat.

In the trip planning stages, it is important to incorporate all facets of a trip. Although the plane ticket to New Zealand costs considerably more than a ticket to Cancun, you might find lodging in New Zealand is less if you opt for a guest house. As much as you want to chase the big bonefish on the west side of Andros Island but scoff at the thought of paying for an all-inclusive lodge, the time you save by not having to research and arrange your own lodging on another island in the Bahamas might save you money in the long run.

The desire to travel to a new location is a natural progression for any angler. So is the desire to buy a boat or other floating craft. Fortunately, in fly fishing that old saw, "The two happiest days for owning a boat are the

If you plan to release more than you keep, a rubber net is a great investment. Entangled flies are easier to remove from a rubber net, and fish don't suffer as much damage to their protective slime.

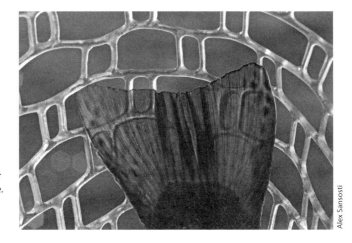

Alex Sansosti

day you buy it and the day you sell it," does not always ring true. The saying is often true for boats with engines on them, but most frugal fly fishers are going to own rafts or drift boats rather than bass boats or flats skiffs.

Rafts, drift boats, canoes, float-tubes, or floating pontoons (individual floating crafts) allow you to access more water. By choosing to purchase

Matt McMeans; www.bighornkingfisher.com

The decision to buy or not buy a boat is a big one. Be honest with yourself in how much you plan to fish, and whether you will be the one rowing all the time.

Matt McMeans; www.bighornkingfisher.com

Before you buy a boat, make sure you have some angling friends who will join you in your floats—fishing from a boat only makes sense if you're with companions.

a boat you are committing to fish a lot more than you already do. *Only purchase a boat if you honestly think you are going to fish twice as much as you do now.* If you're uncertain, consider planning a destination trip or booking several days with a fishing guide instead.

If you plan to fish rivers more than lakes, a raft or drift boat is the best option. If you plan to fish lakes or ponds, a float tube or pontoon is a better idea.

Rafts are more versatile than drift boats, but a drift boat, if cared for, has the potential to last longer. Some of the better raft manufacturers today are Northwest River Supplies, AIRE, SOTAR, and Outcast.

As little as ten years ago, there were very few drift boat manufacturers. Today, there are plenty.

Little Towels: Pack a few little towels. These are great for wiping down gear at the end of the day, or wiping up excess bug dope or sunscreen so you don't get that goop on your fly line. A few little steps increase the life of your gear.

A boat allows you access to water you might not otherwise be able to fish. Here an angler can stay at a favorite run well into the twilight hours.

Clackacraft, Hyde, Lavro, and Willie have been around the longest. There are plenty of other great manufacturers out there making quality boats. Clackacrafts hold their value better than any other boat made today, so consider resale when looking to buy.

If you are still unsure of which type of craft to buy, use the following question-and-answer table to get your results.

1. How many days a year do you fish? Be conservative if you are unsure.
   Less than 10? Go to number 2.
   More than 10, but less than 20? Go to number 3.
   More than 20? Go to number 4.
2. You need to fish more. Keep your money.
3. Do you have any friends that have boats?
   If yes, get to know them better.
   If not, go to number 2.
4. Where do you fish most?
   On rivers? Go to number 5.
   On lakes? Go to number 6.

5. Do you have a truck or vehicle that can haul a boat on a trailer?

   If yes, go to number 7.

   If not, go to number 3.

6. Are the lakes you fish easy to access—in other words, can you drive up to a launch or beach?

   If yes, go to number 8.

   If no, go to number 3.

7. On average, what is the size of the river you fish or would float?

   100 feet wide? Go to number 9.

   200-plus feet wide? Go to number 10.

8. You want a float-tube or oar-propelled pontoon boat. A canoe could also work well. That allows you to load the boat on your car and carry it to the shore and hand-launch.

9. A raft under 15 feet is what you want. This allows you to access the smaller waters and not have to worry about rivers with low flows. A rafter under 15 feet can float well in very small rivers and is easy to portage when necessary.

10. Consider a drift boat if the rivers you fish have enough water in them each season to float. Drift boats must be trailered to every river and can only be used when there is enough water in the river to float safely.

Before you purchase, understand how much time will be needed to learn to maneuver your new boat safely. Then find out how much time it will take to learn how to maneuver it *effectively* for fishing. Rowing a boat to get from the put-in to take-out is one thing, but rowing a boat to effectively fish a river is an entirely different set of skills.

Boats are an investment of time and money. They open up a lot of fly-fishing opportunities for the frugal fly fisher, but they can also be a constant reminder of an impulsive decision based on glamour, not practicality. Like a lot of things important to the

Sunscreen Right After You Shower: When heading out for the day, put sunscreen on just after you towel off from your morning shower. You don't have to waste time applying sunscreen at the boat ramp, and the sunscreen has a better effect.

A raft is more useful than a drift boat when packing gear is important.

Dave McCoy, Emerald Water Anglers, LLC

frugal fly fisher, the choice to buy a boat requires research and restraint, but with the potential for big reward.

Spending money on a professional fishing outfitter or guide is a decision with less at stake than buying a boat. Professional fishing guides make their money on ensuring their clients have an enjoyable experience. If you are considering hiring a guide, there are a few things to consider. First, what do you want out of your experience with the guide? Do you need to learn a new skill that the guide could teach you? Will you catch a lot more fish because of the guide? Is hiring a guide essential to your trip? For example, if you are in Belize, you may have to hire a guide to get you to an area with feeding fish. And lastly, how do you know the guide you are hiring is right for you?

Learning and catching often go hand-in-hand, but before deciding to hire a guide, consider your objectives. If learning is the most important, then the mere act of bringing a fish to the net should not be the most important aspect of the trip. But if all you care about is catching a lot of fish no matter what skills you have, or do not have, then admit that to yourself.

Once you've made a conscious decision on what you want, be sure to communicate that to the guide. A guide is going to approach a day of fishing differently if his clients want to become better anglers than if they want to get as many fish as possible.

Depending on where you are fishing, it may be essential to hire a guide. Many saltwater destinations require the use of a boat, in which case guides are important. For trout fishing, the location, your ability, and your expectations are the main factors in choosing to hire, or not hire, a guide. A lot of trout fishing in the western United States can be done on your own via walk-wade fishing.

A raft can run on smaller rivers even while offering enough room for two anglers.

Garrett Munson; www.montanafishingoutfitters.com

A day spent wading a small stream you found on a map and drove to on your own could be more rewarding than being guided. You found the best holes, you ate your own lunch, you spent time with your dog. When you did catch a fish, you had a greater sense of accomplishment than when the guide holds you by the hand and points you toward the fish.

In spending a day with a guide, you might learn more and will probably catch more fish, and your lunch may or may not be as tasty, but at least you are not eating alone. And you gain the opportunity to get to know a colorful local character who not only knows the fishery like the back of his hand but also has the ability to communicate that knowledge.

But for as many great guides on the rivers, streams, and flats, there are just as many poor guides. So what's the difference between a great guide and a poor guide? With all the guides, outfitters, and fly shops out there advertising their services, how does the frugal fly fisher know which service or guide is the best for them? And what's the difference between a guide, an outfitter, and a fly shop?

Bringing a fish to the net is a culmination of many elements. Fishing guides work very hard to make this happen.

A fly shop is a physical place of business that sells fly-fishing gear and services. Most fly shops offer guided fishing trips. In most states, guides and most guided trips must be licensed and run through an outfitter. An outfitter is a booking agent that handles the logistics of matching a guide to customers. Outfitters are an invaluable tool when booking a fishing guide.

Road-Trip Itineraries: If you're planning a road trip, do it so you never backtrack. Plan your fishing in a loop so you save gas money and time.

Now that you've narrowed your search some, how do you find the right outfitter or guide?

In most cases it's up to the client who is hiring the guide or outfitter.

Know your ability and know what you want from your guide or outfitter. Then be sure to talk one-on-one with your guide or outfitter and see if they share the same ideals. Ask for references of past clients or local contacts, such as local hotels or lodges. If the guide or outfitter doesn't offer references or local contacts, then keep calling guides or outfitters until you find one that does. You can compare prices, but be sure to read all the fine print—some shops or outfitters include some things and not others, and you may not wish to be stuck with a bill for two dozen flies and two leaders at the end of the day.

If you have a great trip, tip your guide well, remember his or her name, and be willing to share it.

Chapter 13

Putting It to the Test: Rod Reviews

Part of the appeal of fly-fishing lies in its simplicity. If you have a line, a rod, a reel, and a fly, you're ready to fish. But as with most modern pursuits, the amount of available gear has grown dramatically within just the last few years. From graphite rods to breathable waders, the frugal angler could spend hours fretting over simple gear decisions. If you are looking for a 4-piece 5-weight rod, there are probably fifty different models and lengths to wade through before you choose one. Tip-flex, fast-action, tapered-bevel, scrimshawed reel sheet . . . As a frugal angler you are willing to spend a little extra time learning about the various makes and models, but not *too* much time. You'd really rather be fishing.

Every-Other-Rule: When adding to your rod arsenal, purchase a rod in a line weight two weights different than what you currently own. For example, if you own a 5-weight, buy a 3-weight or a 7-weight. The difference between a 5 and 6 is sometimes hard to tell and they can be used for similar fishing situations, but the difference between a 5 and 7 is worth having another rod.

Your most significant investment as a frugal fly fisher is going to be your rod. When committing to that purchase, you want to make the most informed decision possible. Given that no one knows fishing gear quite like guides and outfitters (they may not be the best at keeping their lawns mowed or taking down their Christmas lights, but they know the tools of their trade), we asked a number of professionals to help us sift through the current marketplace.

It would be impossible to review all line weights, so we asked them to spend time with various 5-weight rods. A quality 5-weight works for most fish the frugal angler will target and can fish everything from a small trout-filled stream to a large bass lake.

Rods are a specialized angling tool. Like any sports equipment they serve a specific purpose—to help anglers catch fish. When choosing a rod and reviewing rods, it is important to understand the terminology. Here is a brief description of the terms you need to learn to make the best use of the reviews in this chapter.

Casting Stroke. Your casting stroke is the speed at which your rod travels through the air while going from your back-cast to your forward-cast and vice versa.

Rod Action. This is the "feel" of the rod while it moves through the air during your casting stroke. It is also the pace at which the rod must travel during the casting stroke so the rod is able to do the work it was built to do. Rod action is often broken-down into slow, medium, medium-fast, and fast action.

Slow-action Rod. A slow-action rod has more bend throughout the length of the rod. Because of the great bend in the rod, the casting stroke required is slower and more gradual. Benefits of a slow-action rod: Easier for beginners to cast, they are often best suited for situations where a delicate presentation is required, and the greater bend, or flex, of the rod allows for better protection of light tippets. Fighting fish on slow-action rods is a joy because every movement of the fish can be felt through the entire length of the rod and into the handle. There are few slow-action rods on the market today.

Medium-action Rod. With less bend than a slow-action rod, a medium-action rod is a nice middle ground for an all-around rod. They offer a mellow-mix of casting ease and the ability to protect light tippets. In heavy wind or with large flies they might underperform.

Medium-Fast Action Rod. Until about five years ago most rods fell into this category. Rod manufacturers had found the middle ground between a rod that could power through the wind with big flies and a rod that had enough bend throughout the length of the rod to protect tippets, and the fighting of the fish was enjoyable to feel. A medium-fast action rod has little bend of the rod until the last few rod guides. These

This angler puts a good "bend" in the rod while fighting a large trout. Quality rods have a good amount of bend so you can feel the movements of a fish on the end of your line.

rods have a soft-feeling tip—one that protects tippets and is responsive to the movement of a fish on the end of the line. If you were to only own one rod, you want a medium-fast action rod.

Fast Action Rod. With recent technological advances in graphite and other materials (such as boron), fly rod manufacturers are continually pushing the envelope. Today's fast action rods are *fast*. So fast that most anglers do not understand their own casting ability enough to truly get the most out of most fast action rods sold today. These fast action rods are things of beauty and can cast a country mile. They are the equivalent of a Lamborghini, and should probably be used about as often.

Full-wells, Half-wells, and Cigar Rod Handle Grips. These are the shape of the cork on the rod handle. Most rods 7-weight and higher have half- or full-wells grips. Half- and full-wells grips have a beveled upper end of the cork. A cigar grip is smooth on the upper end. Most trout rods are cigar grips, especially rods 6-weight and lighter.

Snake Guides. These lightweight rod guides have a curve to them, allowing the fly line to travel more smoothly through the rod guides.

Most rods today have snake guides, and their popularity is proof of their casting improvement.

Stripping Guides. These are the first few guides on the rod. They are not snake guides. High-quality rods—not *cheap*—should have at least one guide (snake or stripping) for each foot of the rod.

Reel Seat. This is at the butt-end of the rod and holds the reel in place. Choose an up-locking reel seat. There are also wood or aluminum spacers in the reel seat. Try to choose anodized components to your reel seat.

Ferrules. In multipiece rods, which all are today, ferrules are the junction of two pieces. There are several styles and little difference exists between the styles.

Rod Windings. Thread windings that hold the guides on the rod. A quality rod will have plenty of thread wraps and will be well coated with hard epoxy.

Rod Finish. The final coat of paint or protection on the rod. Do not let looks fool you—just because a rod has a shiny, attractive finish doesn't make it better.

Spey Rods. These are two-handed rods, used primarily on larger rivers or very specific fishing situations. As a frugal angler, bypass any spey rods and opt for a more traditional casting rod.

Cordura cases are great, but this case has seen better days. Notice the shrinkage of the Cordura itself. After five years this case is ready for replacement.

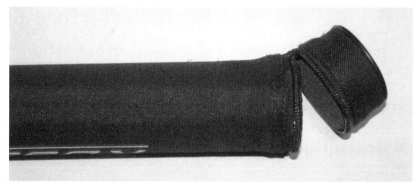

This brand new Cordura reel case is lightweight, small, and a good option for a pack rod or for traveling.

A hard metal case is the best long-term option for any rod. They can be cumbersome and heavy, but they protect your investment.

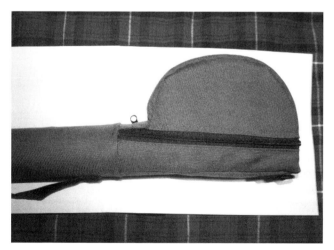

Many manufacturers are making cases wherein the reel can stay attached to the rod. While these are great for short-term usage, do not leave your reel attached to your rod longer than a few days. The added tension placed on the reel seat wears it down faster.

Review Team

The review team for *The Frugal Fly Fisherman* consists of four veteran fly-fishing guides and outfitters. Over the course of one angling season these four anglers fished an assortment of rods from various manufacturers. They also placed the rods in the hands of their clients. What follows is a brief synopsis of each rod fished.

How come only these rods?

The fly-fishing market is saturated with rod manufacturers. From Walmart to local rodmakers, finding a rod isn't difficult—but finding one that fits your casting style and your budget is a tough task. To include all rods and rod manufacturers currently on the market would be cumbersome and redundant. The rods featured are not the only rods on the market today, and as manufacturers utilize new technologies, these models may be out of date in several years. But they will still catch fish—the rods on the market twenty years ago still do a fine job for those fishing them today.

Garrett Munson
Owner, Montana Fishing Outfitters
www.dragfreedrift.com
Homewater: Blackfoot River and the small streams of Montana

Montana Fishing Outfitters; www.dragfreedrift.com

Garrett Munson boasts a Missouri River monster.

Matt McMeans (holding rod) instructs a client on the Bighorn River in Montana.

Matt McMeans; www.bighornkingfisher.com

8.5-Foot Cut-Off: If you fish mostly larger rivers, ponds, or lakes, never buy a rod shorter than 8.5 feet. But if you fish small creeks, never buy a rod longer than 8.5 feet.

Matt McMeans
Owner, Bighorn Kingfisher Lodge
www.bighornkingfisher.com
Homewater: Bighorn River, Montana

Mike Guerin
Owner, Full Circle Outfitters
www.fullcircleoutfitters.com
Homewater: Florida Keys

Full Circle Outfitters; www.fullcircleoutfitters.com

Capt. Mike Guerin holds the results of "just another day in paradise."

Judson Conway (holding the brown trout) and a happy client.

Judson Conway; www.ecoflyfishing.com

Judson Conway
Owner, Elk River Outfitters North Carolina
www.ecoflyfishing.com
Homewater: Rivers and streams of the southern Appalachians

Orvis Clearwater II

Model fished: 905-4 (four piece, 9-foot, 5-weight). Tip-Flex.
Retail price: $198

Orvis has been making the Clearwater series for almost twenty years. Over the past few years they spent considerable time redesigning all of the rods. All reviewers agreed they nailed it. The model fished had a Tip-Flex rating. Orvis gave these rods a beautiful royal blue color. They come with a brushed graphite reel seat insert and an anodized up-locking reel seat. The guides are mid-range quality. Rod comes in a Cordura carrying case. They range in lengths and line weights from 7.6-foot 3-weights to 10-foot 8-weights.

www.orvis.com

Orvis rates all their rods based on the flex, or bend, of the rod. The rating is relevant to casting action of the rod. A Mid-Flex will have a slower casting action. With this rod, the 905-4 Clearwater II Tip-Flex, the casting action was fast, but the redesign created a rod with a subtle tip. All reviewers agreed the rod could cast plenty far for most angling situations. Some liked the softer flex in the tip—they felt the rod's butt and midsections offered good strength to the rod and the softer tip allowed them to really feel the movements of a fish when they were on the line. One reviewer thought a Mid-Flex action might be better suited for a beginner, but he also thought the Tip-Flex model is ideal for an all-purpose rod.

For fighting big fish on light tippets or with small flies, all reviewers agreed that the subtleness of the tip action allowed the movements of the fish to be felt. When fishing small flies, especially small dry flies on long leaders, two reviewers felt the rod a little overpowering—like the rod wasn't quite subtle enough to turn over a 15-foot leader with ease.

But upon setting the hook on a big fish, these two reviewers loved the soft tip because it didn't pop the fly out of the fish's mouth or break it off.

For the price tag the Clearwater II series is as good as they come. This rod has a twenty-five-year unconditional guarantee.

Ross Essence FS
Model fished: 590-4 (four piece, 9 foot, 5-weight)
Retail price: $129

Ross boasts a solid reputation for producing quality reels. The venture into rod-making has proved worthwhile with their Essence FS rods. What these rods lack in aesthetics (they really aren't much to look at), they make up for in performance and price. They have an anodized reel seat and come with a Cordura case. Line weights and lengths range from 7.6-foot 3-weights to 9-foot 12-weights.

All reviewers enjoyed the medium-fast action of the rod, but one reviewer felt the rod didn't fall into the "medium-fast" category. He thought it was too fast to be considered "medium."

www.rossreels.com

They all agreed the Essence FS is an ideal choice for beginners because of its smooth transition from backcast to forward to cast. When put to the test against a stiff wind, the rod was able to cast large salmon flies with ease. One reviewer thought the cast died out at 60 feet, but he also noted there was a stiff upstream breeze.

One reviewer fished a heavy sinking line and the rod responded well. All of the reviewers noted how easy this rod was to cast, but did note that at distances beyond 60 feet the rod was a little less responsive. However, most reviewers agreed that very few trout fishing situations require casts longer than 60 feet.

With the introduction of their Essence FS rod, Ross offers a great rod for the price and a rod that can serve two purposes—an introductory rod and a long-term rod for a wide array of angling situations. This rod has a lifetime unconditional guarantee.

Sage Vantage
Model tested: 590-4; (4-piece, 9 foot, 5-weight)
Retail price: $250

For years Sage has been revolutionizing graphite rod manufacturing. From the ground-breaking RPs and RPLs over twenty-five years ago, Sage's reputation as one of the best rodmakers in the industry is rooted in reality. Their Vantage series offers frugal anglers a serious option for tapping into Sage's technology. Vantage rods come in two- and four-piece models from line weights 3 to 9. They are made with Sage's commitment to quality and durability and feature anodized up-locking reel seats.

www.sageflyfish.com

Out of the case the entire review team was not impressed with the looks of the rod. Before you look elsewhere, a good-looking rod doesn't make you a better caster nor do the fish care if your rod is burgundy or green or brown. But once the reviewers cast, they all agreed the rod's mellow medium-fast action was perfect for learning or for casters who don't buy into the "gotta-have-a-fast-as-possible-rod-action" hype. One review pointed out it is ironic Sage, a company known for the fastest action rods on the market, makes one of the more slower-action intro rods available. The consensus amongst the review team was very positive about the action of the rod. One reviewer enjoyed casting the rod but noted the up-locking reel seat was a little too tight fitting on his reels.

All reviewers agreed the rod handled well at long and short distances. Wind was never a problem; neither were big flies or sink-tip lines. The rod felt light in the hand, responsive to fish on the end of the line, and large fish on light tippets. This time around Sage put some serious thought into an easy-casting and practical fishing rod that was reasonably priced—and they got it right. It has a lifetime unconditional guarantee.

Scott A3
Model tested: 9-foot 5-weight
Retail price: $335

Scott has been making fly rods out of the Montrose, Colorado, location longer than most folks have been fly fishing. With the A3 series Scott boasts their Colorado-made product is unlike other lower-priced rods on the market. And they are correct, because very few rods priced under $350 are made in the United States. A3 rods have a mellow look to them, similar to Scott's higher-priced rods; they are not finished in brilliant colors or feature glossy rod wrappings. They feature an anodized up-locking reel seat. They come with a Cordura case.

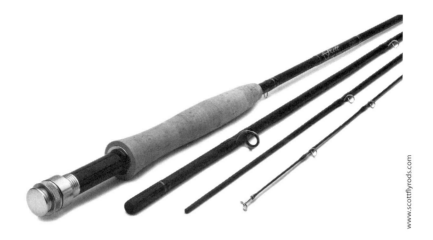

www.scottflyrods.com

All reviewers agreed this rod performed well at close and far distances. Two reviewers felt it was a little heavy in the hand and even clunky when fishing streamers. They suggested, when matching fly line to rod weight, that one should over-line by one rod weight. For example, if using a 5-weight rod use a 6-weight fly line.

One reviewer felt the appeal of this rod lay in how well it did at longer distances. He felt if you were looking for a rod to stick with for a long time, an A3 would be a good option. The tip is soft enough to feel the shakes of a big fish, and the midsection is where the meat of the rod is located—thus the reason big flies are no match for this rod.

Priced considerably higher than other rods tested, the A3 is a good option for a long-term investment. By choosing to purchase a Scott rod, you are also choosing to support a small-town, local business. It has a lifetime guarantee.

St. Croix Imperial

Model tested: I905-4 (four piece, 9-foot 5-weight)
Retail price: $200

Nestled in the deep woods of northern Wisconsin is the St. Croix rod company. It is no coincidence they are located in the same state as the Freshwater Fishing Hall of Fame. St. Croix has quietly been making great fly rods for over thirty years. Their presence in the fly-fishing industry is

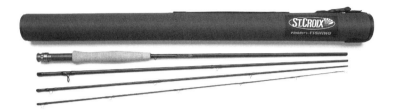

not one of prestige or mass. But for anglers who have been fishing these rods, they have understood one thing: quality rods at very competitive prices. Many anglers who came to fly fishing with a budget in mind have gravitated toward St. Croix rods, and as they invested more time and money into fly fishing, they remained loyal to St. Croix because of the quality and the price.

The model tested was the Imperial series and the entire review team was pleasantly surprised. Although St. Croix has a few lower-priced rod models, for the price the review team felt this model was hard to beat. Imperial rods feature a very attractive burgundy finish, snake guides and aluminum-oxide stripping guides, and a machined aluminum reel seat with a rosewood insert. They come with a rugged case.

The reviewers gravitated to this rod immediately. The case is rugged, but unlike a lot of entry-level rod cases, St. Croix nixed the zipper and created a clip-and-cap system. Two reviewers loved the clip-and-cap system because zippers often break, rust, or fill with dust and when stitched to Cordura cases often become very tight upon wear. The look of the rod, with the deep burgundy color, is appealing to the eye as well, noted one reviewer.

The rod feels light in the hand, coming in at 2.8 ounces, and a few reviewers were skeptical of its ability to handle big flies or a sink-tip. Although the rod action was a little faster, and lighter, than a few of the other rods reviewed, the rod had the backbone to get it done with streamers or big hoppers on a windy day. One reviewer noted that after a full day of fishing the weight proved to be a blessing rather than a curse. The rod had a soft tip to protect light tippets. The review team truly enjoyed fishing this rod. It has a lifetime guarantee.

Winston Passport
Model tested: Four-piece 9-foot 5-weight
Retail price: $199

For 2011 Winston redesigned their entire rod lineup. A few of the old favorites remain, specifically the Boron IImx and the WTs, but for frugal fly fishers your focus is on the lower-priced models. With the introduction of the Passport series, Winston now offers a legitimate rod for under $200. Their Passport series rods are bronze in color, come with high-quality rod guides, an anodized aluminum reel seat, and Cordura case. Rods are only available as four-piece models.

Right out of the tube, all reviewers were happy with the improvement of this rod over its predecessor, the Ascent. This time around Winston put some thought into an entry-level rod. All agreed the color of the rod, a deep, muted bronze, doesn't hold the appeal of Winston's other rods, but in the mind of Winston, spend more cash if you want a rod in their traditional forest green color. Two reviewers said the rod felt relatively light in the hand, although not any lighter than the other models, while the remaining reviewers felt it was a little heavy for a Winston rod.

When fished with a sink-tip line, the rod handled well. When fighting a big fish, all reviewers agreed, the classic Winston "feel" of a softer tip could be felt, and it proved worthy in keeping those big fish on the line, as it protected the lighter tippets. One reviewer felt at casts longer than 70 feet the rod struggled a bit, but if you need to cast any 5-weight longer than 70 feet, then good luck, said another reviewer.

Winston has been making quality rods with a distinct feel for a very long time. The Passport series is their best effort to date—if you ever wanted to own a Winston and wanted to stick to your frugal principles, the Passport series is a great choice. It comes with a lifetime guarantee.

Winston Rod Company

Chapter 14

Real-Life Frugal Fly Fishers: Andy Sabota

Name: *Andy Sabota*

Location: *Driftless area of southern Minnesota, northern Iowa, and southwest Wisconsin*

Blog or website: *www.midwestflyworks.com*

Andy grew up in southwestern Wisconsin, just minutes from one of the greatest concentration of limestone spring creeks in the world. He grew up tugging on the boots of his dad, a professor and semi-professional bass angler, asking to go fishing every chance he could. Andy's love for fishing runs as deep as his Midwest roots. His first day with a fly rod was at

Andy with a smallmouth from a local stream. This fish was caught while fishing from a drift boat—an uncommon sight on most Midwestern streams.

As a kid Andy fished for anything that swam. Smallmouth were abundant near his home.

Andy Sabota: www.midwestflyworks.com

age fourteen, fishing for panfish with poppers. He started tying flies and guiding the local spring creeks at the age of twenty-two to help make ends meet and pay for trips to various locales from Alaska to the Smokies to Florida. He guided out of pure enjoyment and necessity. He describes himself as a perfectionist, tinkering at his vice as much as he can, working on new patterns for the local spring creeks, or tying classic salmon flies. He's a more-than-avid bird hunter and woodworker. He currently teaches chemistry in Lanesboro, Minnesota, while residing on the banks of little Frego Creek. He fishes over two hundred days a year on a teacher's salary. Impressive.

Who, or where from, did you learn the bulk of your fly-fishing skills?
I learned most, if not all, of my general skills from the best teacher on earth—my dad. I think I had some instincts, but he undoubtedly explained to me the idea of reading water, always casting with a target in

mind, the need to practice throwing plugs into ice cream containers, why you should expect a fish on every cast, which I still do, etc.

What about learning skills for fly fishing for trout?
So, when I started fishing trout in the early 90s, the entire skill set was there, maybe not 100 percent, but certainly there. I just needed to hone some fly-casting skills, learn to tie flies, find more water, and most of all, spend more time than any human ever should fishing—much to the dismay of my organic chemistry professor. I worked third shift at the People's Food Coop bakery in La Crosse, Wisconsin, and if I wasn't at the shop, I was fishing. I don't think I slept much.

What, or who, was your biggest motivator?
My biggest fishing motivator might have been a close friend, Dennis Graupe, who owned the local fly shop in Coon Valley, Wisconsin. I learned a lot, and I owe his soul a debt of gratitude that is not fully encompassed by some given set of written words. He was my true fly-fishing mentor if one existed, if for no other reason than he was very good at what he did and shared it all with me and never asked anything in return. I'd stay at his house in the valley for days at a time, month after month. He showed me some water I didn't know about, and he showed me that at age forty, you can still be a kid. He also showed me I didn't want to be a fly shop owner—he was the guy who'd put a sign on his shop door saying GONE FISHING—SUGGEST YOU DO THE SAME. Not a very good way to run a business, but it made for some great times astream.

What level of angler would you rate yourself?
The fly rod did not speak to me at age sixteen, but it spoke loud and clear at age twenty. When discussing how good you are, you typically defer to someone you admire, who is much older, and much wiser. I was pretty good when I was twenty-two, I just didn't have the wherewithal to say it out loud. I think I knew it, and now and then I'd show it, but wouldn't ever stand in line to tell the world that I was some great fly fisherman. I know plenty of people who also catch more fish.

Where might you suggest be the best place for "cheap" or free but useful instruction?

Hands down, a local club. Around here, I don't know of many TU groups that don't have some awfully nice people usually willing to help.

———

Fly-fishing gear is essential to getting out there and enjoying the sport. Today, the manufacturers have nearly drowned most anglers in gear—sifting through the options is a full-time job.

What piece of gear is the most important and why?

For me, my rod. It needs to be a tool, an extension of every fishing-related nerve and synapse I have. Locally, my rod needs to bend to the butt when I ask it to, it needs to be able to roll-cast in pretty heavy cover, rocket launch if I have to, and put a #22 trico on the money at 30 feet if I need it to. Very few rods do that for me, so I tend to be pretty picky. It also depends on where I am, what fish I'm targeting, and what I'm targeting it with.

Do you have any specific rod lengths or weights you like depending on where you are fishing?

If I'm on what I call the big river locally with the boat, that usually means streamers, full sinking lines, and a 9-foot 6-weight or 9-foot 7-weight. I still like it to have a bend in the middle, with a quicker tip, but it needs to load at 20 feet, too. Out west on some of the larger rivers like the Missouri or Yellowstone, I want a 9-foot 5-weight.

What piece of gear is the most overrated—in other words, what piece of gear is it okay to skimp on?

Here . . . in the Midwest, a reel, hands down. The creeks around here are maybe 3 feet wide on the small side, and 15 feet wide on the large side. A lot of the pools in these creeks could double as a very cold Jacuzzi!

Waders are second in line because you can get by with sandals and nylon pants in the summer just fine, and the boot-foot hip-boot was

Waders are important in the Midwest because you have cold water temps in winter and an abundance of muck and biting insects. With all the time spent crawling in the grass, it is nice to have an impenetrable wall between you and the nearest spider or snake.

Andy Sabota: www.midwestflyworks.com

invented for local water that's rarely deeper than 3 feet. I guess the big reason I went to waders other than to have them in the cooler months was that I didn't have to pull smushed corn spiders, caterpillars, and grasshoppers out of my socks anymore. That was gross. I can thank W.L. Gore for fixing that.

What are your three most overlooked pieces of gear, in order of their importance, and give a very brief description of why?
First, the right rod for the job. I don't like fast rods when you don't need them. It's like hunting for squirrels with a .50 caliber. Also, the need to cast 40 feet here is pretty ridiculous. I have my rule of twos . . . let's get twice as close, be twice as accurate, and catch twice as many fish.

Second, polarized sunglasses have to be up there, too. For all that Lee Wulff did, not wearing sunglasses is the one I just can't wrap my melon around. Atlantic salmon on a 3-weight, I'm in. Float planes in Labrador,

I'm in. Having the sun crush my eyeballs . . . count me out. Why, when you have the ability to see the fish, to keep your eyes from getting strained, etc., you wouldn't take full advantage of it I'll never know. A good pair of quality sunglasses isn't going to break the bank either. I wear prescription eyewear, and I largely consider them the most precious piece of sporting equipment I own.

Lastly, the right type of clothing. Avoid cotton. Go for Capilene and synthetics like that. Plenty of layers that can be adjusted to fit the changes of the day if you plan on an all-day event. Food too! You can clip flies to make them smaller, or buggier, or whatever, but it's hard to be warm without that extra fleece coat.

What are your top three gear-related tips to extend the life of your gear?
With hip boots or waders, the need to dry them out after every trip out cannot be over-emphasized. They'll start to get funky in no time at all if left in a hot car. Putting rods away wet will cause them to delaminate.

People have a funny tendency with reels to pull line out backward against the line guard. With some reels, you'll cut into the reel pretty quickly and it gets sharp. It'll also shred lines pretty quickly too.

Lastly, buy a double taper for 90 percent of your fishing. I have a friend who buys them and cuts them in half. He uses a large-arbor reel but smaller line-weight and puts on more backing. A double taper will roll-cast infinitely better, and it is getting two lines for the price of one. In my own opinion for most trout fishing, weight-forward lines are the best scams ever. Even if I have to punch a lot of line, I'd rather have the weight distributed more evenly over the line. It tends to flow better, and in the end there's probably more weight up there to buck the wind.

Do anglers have to sacrifice quality for price?
Buy the best quality gear you can, and that doesn't have to be the most expensive. More importantly, buy gear that fits your needs. If you only plan on fishing three or four days a year, don't buy a $700 rod. Buy something more reasonable . . . and there are a lot more reasonably priced rods out today than perhaps since the early '90s.

For most frugal fly fishers, finding places to fish offers up a whole other set of challenges. When you first started fly fishing, was it hard to find places to fish close to home?

Given that there are something like ten thousand miles of spring creeks in the Driftless area, it was certainly not a problem. To this day, if I even see another car, I keep driving unless I either know the car, or I know which way they went, up or down. So no, it was never that hard. I've never had it tough.

What do you say to folks who aren't as lucky to be so close to so much water?

It's not hard to find places to fish close to home unless home is downtown Cicero in Illinois. But even then, I also think you need to adjust your expectations accordingly, which is why I think a lot of the other species are fished for. If it's between delicately stalking a 6-inch creek chub, grass carp, or popping bugs in a city park or watching your lawn grow . . . I know where I'd be at.

No matter if it was hard or not, how did you find places?

Most of the water, I remembered from when I was a kid in the early '70s when trout fishing was about as popular in the area as disco is now. When I hit full speed in the early '90s, all you had was cheap gas, the Wisconsin, Minnesota, or Iowa trout book, and a *DeLorme Atlas and Gazetteer*. Between all three, you were golden. Today, fuel is more, and you have Garmins. It's a wash. In the Driftless area, you only need to wander. Given that Ted Leeson hit the nail on the head in *Jerusalem Creek* calling the area "miniature," you don't need to wander far to find places. It's a big place and all, but the creeks are everywhere.

What about talking to other anglers or meeting guys from angling clubs?

Word of mouth can get touchy. I know people who literally would blindfold you to take you to a place. I think one of the problems is that secrets are so important that people get protective of "their" water, even though most of it is public.

Growing up in Wisconsin meant Andy was always close to fishy water.

Andy Sabota; www.midwestflyworks.com

What about someone who isn't willing to put in a little "sweat equity" in finding a place?

Your average guy who doesn't fish that much, or is not willing to think outside the box a bit, is stuck with the water everyone else like him has. As a result, you'll see four or five cars at a bridge. It's probably great water, but it's also probably getting pounded. The next valley over may be completely empty. And that might only be a five-minute drive. Having said that, being told about everything does tend to take the fun out of exploration.

You keep talking about all of these spring creeks. I assume a lot of that water is private or hard to access?

The Driftless area has more miles of spring creeks than any other area on earth, so finding a place isn't really much of a challenge as long as you have the DeLorme and an accurate public lands map. Some water is posted, some isn't, but always, always err on the side of caution—trespassing is illegal and gives us all a bad name. Having said that, most landowners are usually more than willing to grant permission when asked. They simply appreciate it.

What sort of fish are you talking about catching in this area?
It won't be 18-inch cookie-cutter fish like you'd find on the Missouri or Bighorn sipping tricos, nor will you find many 18-inch fish at all. What you will find are incredibly spooky 10-inch fish and not much competition—and if you have a #16 orange scud, it'll be money.

In order to fish close to home, did you have to fish for nontraditional species?
I remember the summer of '95, we got into a mess on Mooneye on a river here in southern Minnesota. Some were huge, approaching 17 inches. I think we even landed a state record. Of course it was just a blast. I have targeted them since, but only if you find a big group of them rising in a big back eddy somewhere. They all take dry flies too when they are up.

I'll also fish for Redhorse. When spawning, they go to the shelves below pools and tack up. They love a small crayfish or stonefly imitation, and they would pull a trout around by the tail all day long. I'm doing more and more muskie exploration, too.

Bluegill can be a blast, and no one fly-fishes for them in the Midwest. Find a shallow bay with a 3-weight, and if they are on the feed, you'll get tired of catching them. Think of them as mini permit.

Do you use modern-day tools like the Internet and social networking sites to find places?
I'm pretty much a relic when it comes to technology. These days, I still wander, but after nearly twenty years of trout stream exploration, I have a pretty good arsenal of streams I know well. But hey, finding those places wasn't easy—that's the challenge, it's why you find that club or that person willing to help you get it right.

Do you find yourself doing as much exploring now as you did ten years ago?
You get older, get a house, and time doesn't so much let you wander the way you used to. Like the story of the old bull and young bull. I guess I'm a middle-aged bull now, with a few other hobbies, and the sense to know if I run myself ragged, I don't quite have the six-hour recovery anymore. I don't enjoy fishing alone. And the need to do more of it is diminished by my own sense of mortality. I'd just as soon share the moment. Easily accessible local water makes those moments pretty common when friends show up.

So if you do travel, where do you go?
I've been doing more and more research on Great Lakes steelhead, and it's tough. Most of the information on the Internet is thin, and the state biologists do not know enough to tell you much. Most of the guides who know the best water won't tell, so I guess you're back to filling the tank up and grabbing the *DeLorme*. My only problem is that it's so far away from where I live, I don't get to do it much. I'd rather chase muskies and smallmouth locally, because they are easily accessible and cheap to catch, considering fuel costs.

What is your best story or memory about discovering a new place to fish close to home or a new species close to home?
About ten years ago, my good friend Wayne was up from Chicago. He's a corporate guy who gets to fish when he can, but he's an excellent stick and a phenomenal tyer, so he's always been right at home. In fact I'd say he was my tying and casting coach early on in my fly-tying career.

We're driving down this windy road, and we see a small yellow sign, like what means Department of Natural Resources water in Wisconsin where we used to fish when we were younger and is public water. Not thinking that this was a different state, we pull in, only to find out that this was in fact a sign from the electrical company marking a utility. We had gotten out of the car to read the sign, and we noticed water, a microscopic creek if you will, behind it, gurgling along. We also notice fish scatter through a riffle when we peered over the edge of the bank. We entered the stream, and since it was probably May, there was considerable foliage up, and let me tell you, this place was thick with brush and tight casting. The riffles were maybe 3 feet wide in the wide spots, with overhanging banks with undercuts, and trees everywhere. We still didn't know if there would be trout, but considering that every body of water like this in the Midwest has trout, we weren't really worried. The creek had all the right makings . . . overhead cover, bugs, depth, remoteness etc. It's along a county road, but we didn't see a footprint or telltale path along the creek.

What happened next?

I think I went first, and fished through a small area, making little zip casts into fishy water, and I may have missed a fish, I don't remember. Wayne was up next, and immediately before he cast, I said something to the effect

Small creeks like this one dot the Midwest. It's enjoyable entertainment just finding out which ones contain fly-rodable fish.

Andy Sabota; www.midwestflyworks.com

of, "If you can make that cast, and catch a fish, I'll build you a statue." Ironically, at the same moment he made roughly the same comment but in different words. The cast zipped out, gently settled on the water, and the most beautiful little wild brown trout of about 7 inches ate the fly. He set the hook, and the rest was history. There were a few nice pools of larger size and all had nice populations of wild, beautiful fish. I still fish there at least a few days a year, and have chosen it as the place to close my season each of the past several years. A year later, my wife was doing some frog telemetry studies with her coworker, and mentioned that I was fly-fishing up on that same little creek. He told her it wasn't possible, and that it was just too small to fly fish on.

Did the creek have a name or had anyone ever talked about it?
Probably not. It was too small. When Wayne and I were about at the car, I commented to him, "That's it." He said, "What do you mean, that's it?" I replied, "The creek stops." "Huh?" he said. The whole creek pops right out of the ground in one large discharge of rushing clean water.

What is the best piece of advice for anglers wanting to fish closer to home?
You need two things typically. The first is the time to make it worth it. You might strike out the first fifteen attempts at finding the place you're looking for. You can't quit. You keep going because you don't want to mow the lawn, or rake, or go back to the office. The second thing, and equally importantly, you need to have the fly-fishing skills to make the type of water work for you when you find it. Take the time, practice, practice, practice, and be able to capitalize on it when you find it. Last summer, I had a client out, and it was a particularly slow day, and he was definitely not into the casting groove. About halfway through the day, I asked if he played golf. He replied, "Yes . . . several times a week." I could tell.

The natural progression for a lot of fly fishers is fishing close to home and then venturing to some far-off places. And by far off I mean a day's drive or more, or a flight to get to the destination.

Was it a long time before you invested time and money in a destination trip?

My first destination trip was in the mid-90s to Montana. My dad and I wanted to fish out West after having read the books and seen the articles. I remember we went and more or less got our rear ends handed to ourselves. Very few nice fish, in fact very few fish period were caught other than some small fish on the Gallatin. A few years later I went to the Smokies with my future wife. We went in winter. The weather was great for us, but the locals thought we were nuts. No one was around and we caught some fish. We didn't catch a ton, but we caught some.

Do you think these trips would have been better if you'd invested in guides?
Absolutely.

Have you done any DIY trips in far-off destinations?
I have dreams of Mongolia, but I hate airplanes. I did Alaska for three months for a graduation present. My dad and I fished for seventy-four straight days that summer. We played golf once. I think we had some form of licenses in Minnesota, Iowa, Wisconsin, Montana, Oregon, Washington, British Columbia, the Yukon, and Alaska. Not too bad. We also caught arctic grayling above the Arctic Circle since my dad said they wouldn't be official unless they were over 66.666°.

Are these DIY itineraries something you suggest to frugal fly fishers if they have never been to a destination before?
You bet. You learn a lot and experience more when you are forced to think outside of the box. When you are on your own and it all depends on you, you get a better appreciation for yourself and your abilities. You have to have the right temperament for it. If you know you're type A, and have limited time and need to catch fish to be happy, a DIY event might not be a good idea. Then, maybe you hire someone. If you know you won't be happy unless you catch a bunch of fish, and you have the means to hire a guide, by all means do.

For Andy, like so many anglers, destinations like Montana are locations they long to visit.

For me, I'd always go DIY. I am about as frugal as one could possibly get. I've been to Florida twice, and never to the Keys, but north by Jacksonville, where I have relatives. I've fished there twice. I stop by the local shop, get some info, buy a few flies to say thanks, and head out.

For those anglers that do spend money to travel, what are five tidbits of advice?

1. Set realistic expectations for yourself. If you have never fished before, don't expect a thirty-fish day. Even if you are new to fly fishing, don't expect a thirty-fish day. Set limits with regards to time on the water, and make sure you enjoy the sights and smells and sounds of your trip, too. When it's over, they may be all you have if the fishing was slow. Then again, #1 is for anyone, frugal or not.

2. Don't try to fish everything if you don't need to; park in one place and learn it well. On our first trip to Montana, we spent a day on the Bighorn, a day on the Gallatin, a day on the Madison, a day on the Missouri, and a day on the Beaverhead. We never learned a piece of water. Each day, we had to start over, and while it was fun,

we really didn't catch many fish at all. Had it not been for the nice guy at East Slope Angler's in Big Sky giving up some good info and donating a few hooks for me to tie flies with, we'd have had a much more horrible trip. He recognized that I wanted to tie the flies I'd use, and was generous enough to give a kid a buck in hooks to get him going. And he's seen more of our business ever since than he knows about.

3. Opt for fewer flies that were more generic. I am a fan of presentation. Have maybe a half dozen flies of maybe a dozen and a half patterns and I'd say go smaller when in doubt. Fish don't seem to question small flies nearly as much as they do larger ones. Likewise, if you make some call, and do some specific surfing, and you know you are going to spend three days on the Henry's Fork fishing the green drakes, you don't need to have a bunch of #2 grasshoppers tied for the trip.

4. Have a game plan. I love flying by the seat of my pants as a rule. I remember once driving from the Madison to the Beaverhead to the Missouri in one day's time. That's a lot of windshield time for not a lot of fishing time. I wasn't prepared, and I was too cheap to find a pay phone and call a shop to ask how the fishing was. Granted that was long before cell phones. Having a plan is simply more efficient, especially when it comes to everything non-fishing-related.

5. Bring extra equipment, and be willing to adjust if you need to. I have broken more than one rod or fly line on a trip. The double taper line . . . voila, second line for free. Extra rods if you have them are always nice. If you don't have one, you will want one, and no, it doesn't need to be a $700 spare. Is your spare tire a doughnut tire, or a racing Pirelli? Make sure you can get by and it doesn't have to be pretty.

At what point in your fly fishing development did you choose to invest in a guide?
I have yet to do that. The day may be coming, but I have never had the means to do so. If I went to the Bahamas, I'd think about it, but I hear Eleuthera is about as easy as it gets. If I hired someone, I'd look at it as

an extra rod, or reel, or expenses to another place another time. I have no doubt I'd have caught more fish and saved some trips if I had, but it has never been in the cards.

Since you have not yet hired a guide, what sort of things do you pay for out of necessity?

Typically, the only thing I hire out of absolute necessity is shuttles, but I've been known to hitchhike or find other methods too. There was the time I fished with a buddy in the Flambeau for muskies. Shuttles are hard to find in the north woods, so we stopped in at the Ace Hardware in Lady-smith, Wisconsin, to buy a bike. They were all better than $100, but when one of the guys in the store heard what was going on, he told us he had a bike at home he wanted to get rid of. So we followed him to his house, and sure enough, here is the biggest pile of a bike I've ever seen, but it did work. It was a blue Huffy, with no brakes, no gears, and a half flat tire. It must have weighed 50 pounds. But it was our shuttle for the trip. I left it behind the outhouse at the Nine Mile takeout, and it was gone the next spring when we came back. Then we were back to finding someone for hire, which I'll admit was a lot easier, but not nearly as fun.

Then there was the year I went to fish with Michel Fontaine out of West Yellowstone, a fellow tyer of the classics. While waiting for him, I bumped into a young kid outside of Bob Mitchell's. He wanted to be a guide, didn't have a boat, but wanted some time on the sticks. He rowed me from McAtee Bridge to Ennis, which is two normal floats back to back. The car was parked halfway at Varney, our original destination. We got there, and I bartered with some guy to run my car to Ennis because the kid still wanted to row. I think I gave the driver a half dozen super-cherry salmon flies. I was physically shot shortly past Varney, and the kid wouldn't give up the sticks. I'm pretty ambidextrous to spread the wear, and both arms and wrists were shot the next day. I was a wreck, but a happy one. Point being, barter and shooting the breeze gets you everywhere.

We've talked a lot about gear, guides, and going places. But fly fishing is a lifelong passion. There have to be little things that just take time to learn.

Are there other things, little or big, that frugal fly fishers can do to save some cash but still get great fly fishing?

I don't know of anyone who'd take a big fishing trip without an extra person to defray costs. But keep it simple: You don't want a committee to decide what to do each day. If you stumble on small water, three people may simply be too many unless you like fishing side by side watching half the time. I'd say three max unless you intentionally plan to split into pairs.

I used to sell flies to pay for trips. The summer I went to Alaska, I tied seventy-two dozen flies, which was a lot for a twenty-two-year-old, but it paid for the trip.

Food is a huge cost: Is it a fishing trip, or a tour of pricey Western restaurants? Most of the world works on a price point based on what the market will bear, and food on fishing trips and ritzy bars along rivers is no exception. Yeah, I like to eat out a lot, but beanie weenies by a campfire with a side of Spam works too. Stop at a grocery store and buy groceries. Plan meals for evenings, and have simple things to keep you going all day. Good salami is still cheaper than most packaged food, and it lasts forever in a cooler. I might be speaking blasphemy here, but in some places, you can eat fish too. In Wyoming, I know some place where the locals turn people on to some unbelievable brook trout fishing as long as you promise to kill all you catch as they outcompete the native cutthroat.

Lastly, speaking of . . . fish, don't drink till you can't fish. Is it a fishing trip or a frat party?

As for learning, even with the Internet offering tons of free advice, there are still some great books out there.

What would be your favorite books for learning new techniques or general instruction?

For fishing info, I am a huge Lafontaine fan. Granted, most of it is tying info, but he has plenty of fishing tips too. *Dry Flies, New Angles* is great. Maybe it was just his persona, but he was just such a genuine person and it came through in his books. For chucking big uglies, my friend Kelly Galloup's *Modern Streamers for Trophy Trout,* cowritten with Bob Linsenman. There's also a few books locally, written by Ross A. Mueller: *Fly*

When planning a trip, be sure to have one of your best companions along!

Andy Sabota; www.midwestflyworks.com

Fishing Midwestern Spring Creeks—Angler's Guide to Trouting the Drift-less Area; *Upper Midwest Flies That Catch Trout and How to Fish Them: Year-Round Guide.* They are very good books for local information, and Ross is a true gentleman among anglers. Another option is seek out a cool store owner and buy him a beer. There is no better lubrication for fishing info than a well-thought-out bribe.

Other than that, I'm so much more a doer than a reader. I will pick up tidbits here and there, but I prefer to figure it out through friendships or through hard work. I will always call people I know have been to a place before I go someplace I have not been.

181

Andy fishes far-off places on a budget—saving money and time and catching plenty of fish.

You learned a lot about fishing from your father. You put that to good use when you began exploring on your own. Granted, you grew up within a stone's throw of some great trout water; however, you and your dad still ventured far off for fishing. You've seen a lot of changes in fly fishing over the past twenty years. What do you think is missing in the sport of fly fishing?
There are so few twenty- and thirty- and forty-year-olds. So I guess my thoughts are based on where kids should go for help, not necessarily adults. I personally feel if a kid calls me, that a lightning bolt would come out of the sky and strike me dead if I didn't help. It's really just a continuation of my day job. Here's a kid who'd rather learn about fishing than play Nintendo? And I'm going to treat it like a guided trip and charge? Heavens no. Maybe if his dad was a neurosurgeon with a disposable income and a nice Beemer, but here in the Midwest, it's usually a farm kid. And besides, I might get to go chase pheasants on their back forty or CRP if I'm lucky.

Index

Italicized page numbers indicate illustrations.

Smeraglio, John, 85
snake guides, *35*, 152–53
social networking, 8–9, 50, 54–55, 88, 90, 92, 125, 128, 170
socks, 47–48
Soft-Hackles, 66
Southeast locations, 111–13, *112*
Southwest locations, 116–18, *117*
spey rods, 153
split shot, *15*
spools, 41
spouses, 79
St. Croix Imperial (rod), 161–62, *162*
streamers, 66, 67
strike indicators, *15*
stripping guides, 153
sunglasses, *21*, 21–22, *22*, 89, *89*, 126, 168–69
sunscreen, 145
Swisher, Doug, 83

tackle, terminal, 4, 16. *See also specific types of tackle*
Tarpon (DVD), 85–86
tippets, *13*, 13–14, 16, 88
towels, 143
travel, 52–54, 94–96, 132, 135, 137–41, *173*, 176–78
trespassing, 108
trout, 82, 84, 180–81
Trout Unlimited, 76, 77

Valdene, Guy de la, 85
vests, 23, 24

waders, 1, *18*, 18–19, *20*, 21, 25, 167–68, *168*, 169
Walton, Izaak, 102
water bottles, 89
Whitlock, Dave, 82
Why Fly Fishing (DVD), 85
Winston Passport (rod), 163, *163*
Wulff, Joan, 84, 85

About the Author

The author of four books (including *The Orvis Pocket Guide to Streamer Fishing,* Lyons Press, 2006, and *Montana on the Fly: An Angler's Guide,* Countryman, 2008) Patrick Straub has been a fly fishing guide and outfitter in Montana for over ten years. He serves on the board of the Fishing Outfitters Association of Montana and is active in statewide fishing functions.

Stephen Weisberg

This may look like a cheesy grip-and-grin photo of the author holding a small trout. However, look closer and you will see a lot going on: sun protection with sungloves; proper layering for comfort and warmth; and the paring down of gear into pockets.